"The concept alone sold me on Kim's book. There is a desperate need for relational discipleship. It is the most effective way to win people and build disciples. Add to that Kim's practical advice and compelling stories, and you have the recipe for life-changing relationships."

KEN DAVIS
Speaker, Comedian,
Author of *Fully Alive: Lighten Up and Live - A Journey that Will Change Your Life*

"I love this book, and I love Kim Aldrich. She is absolutely the real deal, and what she has poured into this book isn't theory. It's her life! Her transparency and deeply held desire to help others is evident on every page. If you're ready to be more 'others centered' and have been aching for someone to show you how, this is the book you need. In *DiscipleSips*, Kim has poured out a giant mug of wisdom and action points. All we readers need to do is take a sip."

TEASI CANNON
Author of *My Big Bottom Blessing: How Hating my Body Led to Loving my Life* and *Lord, Where's My Calling? When the Big Question Becomes a Big Distraction*

"This book is truly delightful! I was planning to glance at it and come back to it later, but I was immediately drawn in and had to sit down and read through all the chapters. It's engaging, funny, helpful, and inviting—like a pumpkin-spice latté on a crisp fall day. It's also everything a first-time discipler needs—Scriptural truth, real-life stories, relational tools, and down-to-earth conversation starters—plus an experienced coffee-date discipler to walk you through the process!"

KIM AVERY
MA, Professional Certified Life Coach

"In its simplest form, a disciple of Jesus is one who lives like, loves like, and obeys like Jesus. In *DiscipleSips*, my friend Kim Aldrich serves up a wonderful blend of Scriptural truth and practical insights that enables followers of Jesus to become fruitful disciples and effective disciple-makers."

DAVE BUEHRING
Founder & President of *Lionshare*,
Author of *A Discipleship Journey* and *The Jesus Blueprint*

"*DiscipleSips* makes leaving a Jesus legacy as simple as coffee and friendship. If I'd known it was that simple, I would have started years ago!"

MONICA SCHMELTER
Speaker, Host of *Bridges* television show,
Author of *Right Sizing Your Life* and *Does This Make Me Look Fat?*

"Latte and friends—how perfect is that? Life can get tough, but it is more bearable with good friends, a lot of coffee (even decaffeinated), and a book filled with heart-to-heart encouragement and hope, like this one from my friend, Kim Aldrich."

MARTHA BOLTON
Emmy and Dove-nominated Author of 80+ books

"If you've ever wondered how you can make an impact on the next generation but were too scared to take the first step, this book is for you. It provides a simple, approachable way to disciple others in this complicated, chaotic world, and who doesn't love coffee? Kim is relatable and uses real-life examples from her own journey to help you start yours."

KERRI POMAROLLI
Comedian (*Comedy Central, ABC, NBS*), Actress,
Author of *Mom's Night Out and Other Things I Miss*

"In an age when Google will find you the recipe, Alexa will order the ingredients, and YouTube will show you how to make the pie, there remains a vital human role in Christian discipleship that cannot be outsourced or digitized. An apprenticeship in the faith is a face-to-face hands-on relationship, and is not something to be left to the experts and professionals. Kim Aldrich shows us that effective disciple-making can be as natural as chatting with a friend over coffee."

RAMON PRESSON
Marriage and Family Therapist,
Author of *When Will My Life Not Suck? Authentic Hope for the Disillusioned*

"Kim Aldrich is a powerful writer with a heart for discipleship, service, and reaching young believers with practical tools and resources to empower them to live a life of faith and joy."

DR. NAIMA JOHNSTON BUSH
Author, Coach,
Host of *The Refreshing Life with Naima (therefreshinglife.com)*

"Kim Aldrich hits a home run by reaching into the deepest areas of our hearts where we long for a close and trusted friend we can do life with. Her writing, examples, and humor will make you naturally connect with her as you smile, laugh, and dig deeper into areas of your life that help you grow and pass that growth along to others. Just like a fresh-brewed cup of coffee, I find this book so refreshing and good for my soul that I will recommend it to everyone I know."

ROSEMARY FISHER
Author of *Recycled Women, Broken Hearts Have No Color*, and *The Smokin "HOT" Bride of Christ*

"God instructs us to support and love each other. Kim Aldrich's book, *DiscipleSips*, is a beautiful blueprint, a guide to mentoring a thirsty generation. We all have something that someone else needs. Imagine with me, what if every Christian discipled just one? Our next generation would be a pleasing aroma to the Lord. *DiscipleSips* makes it as easy as sharing a cup of coffee."

SUE Z. MCGRAY
Regional Director of *Christian Women in Media*,
Author of *Becoming Visible, Letting Go of the Things That Hide Your True Beauty*

"I worked in coffeeshops for seven years, working my way through college, and I've been in the ministry of making disciples for twenty. So I've made a lot of coffee and disciples. I've also read every book on discipleship I can find, and have heard many theories on what discipleship should look like. We need more books like this that move out of theory into the practical. I highly recommend it to any woman who loves Jesus and wants to make disciples."

JIM HARRIS
Life Groups Pastor, *Grace Chapel,* Franklin, TN,
Creator of *The E3 Challenge* and podcast *(e3challenge.net)*

"Kim is a vivacious, fun, and compassionate woman who's experienced the freedom of Christ and freely shares it with others. Her passion to share the journey of walking with Jesus in such a personal, intentional, and consistent way with others is a model to be followed and meets the desperate need of a generation longing for connection and significance. If you're without a working plan for discipling others, this book is a good place to start."

KEITH MARTENS
Founder and President of *Kingdom Ministries,*
Author of *A Field Guide for Followers of Christ*

"Kim Aldrich has written a must-read for anyone who wants to understand the heart of becoming a discipler. *DiscipleSips* is not just a book—it's a breakthrough that will inspire you to go deeper in your relationships with others. Kim's savvy style will move you from a place of hesitance to confidence as you courageously follow the call to go and make disciples!"

KRISTIN FRANKS
Speaker, Life Coach, Counselor, Author of
HeartBrakes: Navigating Your Way Through Divine Detours, Delays, & Dead Ends

"Kim's writing is a beautiful reflection of her personality—genuine, positive, fun, and endearing—guaranteed to inspire, motivate, and encourage her readers. I can't wait to sit down with a friend, a cup of coffee, and *DiscipleSips*."

PAULA RUSSELL
Founder of *Set Free From Me Ministry*, Author of *Set Free From Me*
and *The Pastor Driven Wife*, Co-Pastor of *New Life Christian Center*, Newport, KY

"In the Word, we're told to go and make disciples. Experience is our greatest teacher. Kim has been there, and she uses her experiences for our benefit...she's been mentored, she's mentored others, and now she teaches us how to mentor. She shares in a very non-threatening, practical, and humorous way that helps break down walls and build trust, so that we too want to carry the mantle of mentor and walk with those He puts in our lives. Grab a cup of coffee, pull up a chair, and sit for a few moments to be discipled in 'friendship discipleship.' "

DR. MICHELLE BENGTSON
Neuropsychologist, Speaker, Author of
Hope Prevails: Insights from a Doctor's Personal Journey Through Depression

"In *DiscipleSips*, Kim Aldrich shares practical encouragement and tangible steps we all can share with younger believers who are hungry for a closer relationship with Jesus. Younger believers need the truth, and this book is full of truths you won't want to miss. Kim takes the reader on an honest and life-changing journey through each story and conversation. Pull up a chair and grab your cup of coffee and a friend, as Kim inspires and encourages you to leave a legacy...one latte at a time."

JAYME HULL
Speaker, Podcast Host,
Author of *Face to Face: Discover How Mentoring Can Change Your Life*

"Kim Aldrich takes discipleship to the next level! *DiscipleSips* is a must-read for all of us! Mentoring for Christ is a mandatory art that has not been scribed in a book with such love until now. The tools she shares are a required read for these end times. Purchase your copy today and share the love of Christ in a joy-full, friendly style!"

KEVA RENEE OTUNUYA
Author,
Podcast Host of *Encouraging Moments with Keva Renee and Friends*

"Kim Aldrich creatively shares her experience and passion for loving and leading others in their relationship and growth in Christ. *DiscipleSips* is full of helpful principles that are easy to read and apply to your life and friendships."

DR. KRISTI GAULTIERE
Spiritual Director/Mentor, Blogger *(SoulShepherding.org)*

"Kim Aldrich has impacted many women through discipleship. Our connection was immediate, as we shared the same passion and excitement for investing the gospel in women's lives. Kim spoke and shared her expertise with our *Women 2 Women* mentors, and the relational and biblical training she provided was both helpful and encouraging. Now that the book has come to fruition, it will be a wonderful tool and an inspiration for women who are seasoned mentors, as well as those who are considering mentoring for the first time. Kim's witty, creative style is so engaging that I believe *DiscipleSips* will become a standard for women who love to help other women grow in their relationship to Jesus."

NANCY BUCK
Leader of *Women 2 Women Mentoring*,
Brookwood Church, Greenville, SC

"Encouraging, equipping, and empowering new believers in Christ is our life-long quest to build lives of maturity, power, and purpose. Kim Aldrich gives practical tools to make discipleship intentional and fun."

SUE DETWEILER
Radio Host, Pastor, Author of
Women Who Move Mountains: Praying with Confidence, Boldness, and Grace

"Every woman has a story. This book cheers each woman to live out her story alongside someone else—someone who needs to be encouraged in her destiny and her walk with Jesus. Kim's book gives practical tools for discipling and expresses the heart of God for living the gospel."

ELIZABETH HUTCHISON
Media Specialist, *Grace Christian Academy,*
DiscipleSips "pilot group" participant

"Discipleship always seemed a little intimidating to me, and even though I knew I'd love to do it, I never really knew how. *DiscipleSips* is so clear, practical, and delightful—it gives real 'boots on the ground' to making the disciple-discipler relationship a reality. I love it!"

SANDY BROWNLEE
Playwright, Author, Transmedia Storyteller,
DiscipleSips "pilot group" participant

"I have a heart for discipling women, but I haven't known how or where to begin. Thankfully, in *DiscipleSips* Kim provides a practical field guide that allows me to cover a comprehensive list of 'mentoring milestones' or single out particular areas of growth—depending on the individual needs of those I disciple. Learning from Kim's experiences and receiving her sound advice gives me confidence going forward that I'll be able to enjoy mentoring relationships, help younger disciples set realistic goals, and avoid common pitfalls and burnout. I am truly thankful to have been able to participate in learning and practicing the *DiscipleSips* tools that are part of this book!"

KELLEY BOYD
Real Estate Agent,
DiscipleSips "pilot group" participant

DiscipleSips

Leaving a Jesus Legacy One Latte at a Time

A Sip-By-Sip Guide to Friendship Discipleship

KIM ALDRICH

Selah Press PUBLISHING

DiscipleSips: Leaving a Jesus Legacy...One Latte at a Time

Copyright © 2017, Kim Aldrich

ISBN-13:978-0692952733 (Selah Press)
ISBN-10: 069295273X

Printed in The United States of America
Published by Selah Press, LLC, selah-press.com
Editor: Anna Floit
Cover Design: Christine Dupre

Unless otherwise noted, Scripture quotations are taken from **the New International Bible®
(NIV),** The Holy Bible, New International Version ®, NIV ®, Copyright 1973, 1978, 1984, 2001 by
Biblica, Inc.™ Used by permission. All rights reserved. Scripture quotations marked **MSG or The
Message are taken from The Holy Bible, The Message.** Copyright© 1993, 1994, 1995, 1996,
2000, 2001, 2002 by NavPress Publishing Group. Used by permission. All rights reserved.
Scripture quotations marked **NASB or New American Standard Bible®** (NASB), Copyright ©
1960, 1962, 1963, 1968, 1971, 1972, 1973, 1975, 1977, 1995 by The Lockman Foundation. Used
by permission.www.Lockman.org. *Holy Bible,* **NLT or New Living Translation,** copyright ©
1996, 2004, 2015 by Tyndale House Foundation. Used by permission of Tyndale House
Publishers, Inc., Carol Stream, Illinois 60188. All rights reserved. *The Holy Bible,* **English
Standard Version (ESV)** is adapted from the Revised Standard Version of the Bible, copyright
Division of Christian Education of **the National Council of the Churches of Christ in the U.S.A.
All rights reserved. The Net Bible® (NET), New English Translation** copyright © 1996 by
Biblical Studies Press, L.L.C. Net Bible® is a registered Trademark The Net Bible® logo, service
mark copyright © 1997 By Biblical Studies Press, L.L.C. all rights reserved.

CONTENTS

EXPERIENCING MY STORY

EMPOWERING YOUR STORY

ENCOURAGING HER STORY

EMBRACING GOD'S STORY

To Mama Margie,
a daughter of the Most High God
and spiritual "mother in the house"
who loved me like I was her own
and cheered me on from heaven
long before she left this earth;
even now I hear her voice
calling me, calling you
across the
finish
line

ACKNOWLEDGEMENTS

When you write a book about *friendship discipleship*, it's only natural to find yourself with quite a few folks to thank. Over the past four years of writing this book, some amazing people have walked alongside me for short or long stretches of the journey—for which I'm eternally grateful.

My heartfelt gratitude goes to...

Kristin Franks: Without you as my accountability partner, this book would still be "almost done." Your consistent check-ins, empathetic heart, and sacrificial friendship have been a rudder for my writing and a salve for my soul in the midst of the grueling process that publishing can often become. You are a treasure—and your book is next!

Dana Russell: The year we spent working on our books together was definitely a "God thing." Rarely have I felt so heard and in sync with another person, like two grown-up five-year-olds having the time of their lives just being themselves together. Thank you for believing in me as my precious "tandem" friend. (your book is coming too...)

Elizabeth Hutchison, Amy Benn: Each of you rolled up your sleeves and dug into the manuscript when I needed your help—Elizabeth by doing multiple read-throughs and Amy by assisting with some of the redline edits. Thank you for your "going the extra mile" brand of friendship.

Nancy Buck, Meredith Edwards: Your kindred-spirit passion for mentoring, for this book, and for using my (at the time) untried materials still amazes me. It's been a joy to help train your *Women 2 Women* mentors and partner with your wonderful ministry—also thank you, Dana Russell, for introducing us. I look forward to many years of shared friendship and fruitfulness.

Steve Berger: Thank you for preaching God's Word with such passionate persistence, and allowing me to use selected content by permission.

Christine Dupre, Kayla Fioravanti, Anna Floit, Lindsey Hartz: Christine, thank you for so patiently working with me to create a gorgeous book cover I absolutely love. Kayla, thank you for overseeing the details of the internal design with unflappable persistence and skill until the absolute eleventh hour. Anna, I appreciate your elegant edits and your flexibility to flow with my grammar "exceptions." Lindsey, thank you for giving me a strategy for launching these words into the world and for running the book launch so I could focus on connecting with readers.

Priscilla Hundley, Margie Houmes: Deep thanks to my beloved mentors Priscilla and Margie for cheering me on (each in their turn) through some extremely tough seasons of the creative process. Most of all, thank you for constantly reminding me who God is, who I am in Him, and what I've been called to—regardless of the obstacles I face in any given moment.

My husband Paul: You have encouraged, supported, listened, coached, nudged, assisted, facilitated, helped with, born with, and prioritized this project in countless ways that no one else but God and yours truly will ever fully know. In particular, your redline edits to pare down the manuscript made a huge difference in flow and readability. Whatever fruit the Lord brings from this book, I pray it will be credited to *your* account as well as mine. It's an honor to be your wife and "do life" together.

I'm also grateful to...

- Every beloved mentor who took the time to invest in me when she didn't have to—it's been an honor.

- Every precious woman I've been able to walk alongside in the name of Jesus—it's been a privilege.

- My own mom, Susie, who led me to Jesus when I was eight years old—which opened the door to everything in this book.

- The beautiful "pilot group" ladies who invested three months of their lives bonding with each other, learning the *DiscipleSips* principles, and providing me with invaluable feedback.

- All those who participated as "book club readers" or *DiscipleSips* Facebook group readers before the book was published.

- Everyone who prayed for me over the past four years—asking God to give me energy, encouragement, wisdom, or writing mercies—or storming the gates of hell on my behalf.

- My fellow writers in the Writer's Circle online group who have so faithfully cheered me on for the past three years.

- Anyone who ever said, "Wow, I need that book" or "I can't wait til it comes out!" Your words encouraged me more than you know.

Most of all, I want to thank the Master Discipler—Jesus. *This book is because of You, about You, and for You.* You, the Father, and the Spirit are my heavenly family, closer to me than my very breath, and I am so in love with You. Thank you for loving this brokenhearted girl into ever-increasing wholeness, joy, and Jesus legacy.

I am beyond grateful.

FOREWORD

Years ago, I saw a Helen Hunt movie about a twelve-year-old boy whose "pay it forward" social studies project made a huge impact on his community. This phrase perfectly describes what we're called to do as disciples of Jesus—freely pour into the lives of others we what have freely received.

Almost thirty years ago, my life was changed and enriched through the life of Sheryl Fleischer, my faithful discipler. As I recall how she loved me, shared her life with me, and imparted her desire to know God and make Him known, I understand more clearly the spiritual legacy I've been privileged to be part of ever since. I caught her vision, and my heart yearned to give to others what I had been given: *The daily habit of journeying with Jesus and a burning passion to pour into other women.*

Many years later I had the privilege of pouring into Kim Aldrich as her discipler. During that year we met in His Presence together, her life and gifts opened like a beautiful rose that has continued to blossom and grow ever since.

Yet this journey of making disciples is not a one-way street of teacher and student; it is a divine exchange. Abba's love molded us both in relationship with each other, a process that continues to this day as we "do life" together.

Yet not all discipleship is accomplished during a weekly meeting with an open Bible and cup of coffee. Much of our lives are spent practicing His Presence quietly, moment by moment, as we learn to receive and radiate His light in our everyday world. It's all part of becoming more like Him, and an essential part of that journey is inviting others to walk alongside us.

Kim is one of my spiritual daughters who is *paying it forward.* Her life is one of daily loving Jesus, her husband, and the women she's been drawn to—those who hunger and thirst for a deeper connection with God and a more tangible sense of kingdom purpose.

In the pages that follow, she will share stories of various women she's been privileged to serve and grow alongside, as both disciple and discipler.

Each of their lives has been branded by greatness through learning to embrace the identity, intimacy, and legacy Jesus offers. They have become a treasured part of her life and family—and through her, they have become part of my spiritual heritage as well. I am blessed and thankful to count them among my spiritual granddaughters.

In this book, *Kim invites you to believe that your life is a gift God has given you to share with other women.* Over time she has discovered a deep well of experience that she offers for your refreshment. It includes simple truth-filled ways of thinking and living, and an invitation to dive into the rich waters of relationship with Jesus and each other. It's a win-win choice for everyone. *You gain and become enriched as you pour yourself out to someone else.* The book of Proverbs says, "He who waters another man's garden is watered himself." It's a spiritual principle.

I know that who I am today, and who Kim has become, is because of Jesus' patient love and willingness to tenderly transform us as we spent time in His Word and His Presence with another beautiful one such as you.

Almost three decades have passed since I was loved and shaped by Truth with a warm, safe person named Sheryl. The passion for discipleship, first hers and then mine, has stood the test of time. I've had the privilege of investing in others along the way, including learning to love and disciple our own children and grandchildren in a lifestyle of giving away what's been given to them.

The desire to see women through His eyes, while understanding my own limitations, has brought a sense of direction for me. Nothing is more valuable than giving your life away for a cause that will last and be multiplied.

Welcome to the adventure called discipleship. My story and your story count, and someone is waiting to hear it. You are loved, you are special, and you too have the commission to go and make disciples.

Priscilla Hundley
February 23, 2017

PREFACE

A joyful heart is the inevitable result
of a heart burning with love.
MOTHER TERESA

If you are reading these words, rest assured it is NOT by accident. For the past several years, you have been on my heart, my mind, and my urgent to-do list—ever since God dropped the idea for this book deep into my spirit.

What began as a whispered wish has grown into a full-fledged longing for you to experience the overflowing abundance Christ died to give you. Because at the risk of sounding blunt: *Nothing else will satisfy*.

I began writing these words because I sensed a desperate need for the church to return to a *lifestyle* of discipleship. As someone who had "stumbled" into the process a decade earlier, I was constantly meeting more young women in need of a mentor than I could ever personally invest in.

I also noticed a pattern in their circumstances. Though many of them were part of a church, Bible study, or even a small group, they continued to feel lost in their own lives. They couldn't quite figure out how to *apply* all they were learning to their actual daily experience, and they felt *alone* in the process. Though they had no language for it, their hearts were longing for *the relational enzyme of discipleship*.

I also saw what a life-changing difference it made to start meeting with them one by one, and watch Jesus do the rest! Soon I was gushing to all my girlfriends about the joys of being a "press-enter" mentor, and (at first) they greeted my news with great enthusiasm.

Yet one by one, as if reading from an invisible script, they uttered the same sad sentence: *But I could never do it*. The more I heard this answer, the more baffled I became. Why did so many mature Christian women, most of whom had walked with Jesus for years or even decades, feel ill-equipped to invest even the most *basic* principles of the gospel in a younger believer?

Heartbroken and confused, I asked the Lord to show me why. And over time, two unmistakable answers rose to the surface.

The first answer was simple.

Because no one's ever taught them how.

Somehow, the simple-yet-powerful practice of one person imparting the life of Christ to another hasn't been passed down from generation to generation.

Instead, we've made it a class—or a program—both of which are beneficial in their place. Yet no class or program, regardless of how powerful, can replace the heart connection of one person supporting and loving another through the process of becoming more like Jesus.

And that's the part many of us have missed. We've learned to be sponges rather than funnels. So naturally, we feel ill-equipped to pour into others.

The second "why not?" answer went even deeper.

Because no one ever discipled *them.*

Unless you've seen the process up-close and personal, how can you know what authentic spiritual mentoring even looks, smells, or tastes like?

My heart aches for the millions of women who still long for another believer to get to know them, love them, and help them master the basics of the faith. Instead, several generations of spiritual orphans have grown up in a silent epidemic of neglect. Small wonder why the church is finding it so difficult to reproduce herself in the next generation!

Over the past four years, as I've poured my heart into this manuscript, this simple how-to guide has grown into something far deeper. It's become a heartfelt expression of love to every woman who's ever longed for a spiritual mentor—or wished she could pass that experience on to someone else.

Every Ruth looking for a Naomi. Every Timothy looking for a Paul. Every beloved disciple of Christ waiting for a Jesus-with-skin-on helper to train her up—and send her out!

Is it possible to walk deeply with Christ without a spiritual mentor?
Absolutely.

Does God take some of us down lonesome roads for His greater purpose?
Without a doubt.

Yet is it His will for most believers to grow up as spiritual orphans because no one's ever taken the time to personally invest in them?

Everything within me cries a resounding "No!"

Why?

- Because of Jesus' last words on earth.
- Because of His personal example with the disciples.
- Because of Paul's investment in Timothy, and Naomi's in Ruth.
- Because of my own experience of spiritual nurture, both given and received.

And because of the look I see in the eyes of women of all ages who long for something more—and I know that "more" is just a step of faith away.

So, if you're tired of going through the motions and ready for adventure, I hope you'll take this journey with me. I believe God wants to fill your cup to overflowing with more good things than you could possibly imagine. It would be a privilege to help you get started, by pouring into your cup what Jesus has poured into mine.

Only He has the deeply satisfying blend of truth, love, and authentic connection your heart is thirsty for. Yet as you learn to drink deeply, you'll be **empowered** and **enabled** to share that same live-giving blend with others. I love you already—and can't wait to get started!

Your fellow disciple-in-training,

Kim

INTRODUCTION

What's Coffee Got to Do with Discipleship?

Some of you may be wondering, *Besides the catchy book title, what's coffee got to do with discipleship?*

**Coffee is a caffeinated substance
used (and abused) by millions of people
to make it through the day.**

**Discipleship is a truth-and-love process
embraced (or neglected) by millions of believers
who want to live the "Jesus way."**

Despite their obvious differences (for starters, I've never seen a drive-thru discipleship window), the two do have one thing in common.

Relationship.

While drinking coffee alone is certainly *possible*—and first thing in the morning, maybe even *preferable*—the current coffeeshop craze strongly suggests that most of the time we prefer sipping our caffeinated concoctions in the company of others.

As it turns out, the same is true of discipleship. While it's *possible* to learn theology from classes, books, or even online, the fact is, human interaction *sweetens* the experience like nothing else. In-person discipleship adds a *relational enzyme* to the process that simply doesn't happen with information alone.

Jesus intended making disciples to include...*other disciples!* And chatting comfortably over a cup of coffee is a great way to add that relational enzyme into your God-conversations with younger believers.

Plus, coffee and discipleship are both better and richer when you linger over them. Poorly brewed coffee is a waste of water. And unlived truth is a waste of knowledge.

Yet drinking deeply of God's ways together, through meaningful conversation and friendly follow-up, allows us to more fully experience the robust, flavorful way of life Jesus came to give us!

Before we dive into this subject, here's a working definition to get us started.

Discipleship is the relational process
of helping a younger believer "press enter"
on her relationship with Jesus so she can experience
the full-circle transformation He died to give her!

Also, just to be clear, whenever you read the terms *mentor/mentoring* in this book, they're always referring to *spiritual mentoring/discipleship*.

The cry of my heart is to be overflowing with so much of God's goodness that it can't help but spill over into the lives of others. If that's the cry of your heart, then grab a cup of coffee and let's get started—*cuz this book is written especially for you!*

FIRST COFFEE CHAT

Experiencing
My Story

COFFEE CHATS

Four Conversations to Fill Your Cup

Have you ever noticed how a simple story can make or break your day?

A friend texts: "Yikes! Just heard that sleeping on ur side makes ur face age quicker! Woman's face on video droops waaaaaay to the left..." Suddenly your day is off and running in a whole different direction.

(most likely to YouTube—or the pillow or skincare aisle)

Later that day, *another* friend tells you about a recent heart-wrenching experience and how amazingly God has turned that situation around for good in her life. As her story unfolds, your own backpack of troubles grows lighter by the moment.

(including your newfound fear of asymmetrical aging!)

Stories are powerful. They draw us in. They also draw us out of our own experience and into someone else's for a much-needed dose of clarity, hope, or "I never thought to be grateful for *that...*" perspective.

A FRESH LOOK

One of the reasons God gave us the gift of storytelling is to allow us to imagine a new experience we've never had, or a kind of life we've never lived—*without even needing to leave home.* Stories provide mental on-ramps and off-ramps to help us visualize the difference between the road we're currently on and another road we might *prefer* to take.

Quite the invention on God's part!

Imagine how dull life would be if you never had the opportunity to look over someone's else's shoulder, learn from her experience, or ponder new possibilities. Hearing other women's stories can shed much-needed light on our own. Because sometimes we're so close to the narrative God's writing through us, we don't even *recognize* it as a story.

Oh, that's not a story...that's just my life!

Yet every believer's story (yes, *even yours*) is handwritten by God to reveal another part of His wonderfully multi-faceted heart. A glimpse of Him that *you and you alone* were designed to reflect in all of history.

JUST GIRLS TALKING

If I had my druthers, we wouldn't be limited to the printed page at all. We'd be sitting down for a cozy cup of coffee—or tea or smoothie or whatever yummy beverage you love best.

Can't you just picture it?

You'd walk in, place your order, and find a comfy table. Pretty soon I'd spot you in the crowd and wave hello.

This coffee date's been on our calendar for weeks, and we're both super excited. After hugs and smiles, I'd dive on in.

"I can't *wait* to tell you what God's been doing lately!"

"No kidding? Spill it!"

And the conversation would be off and running.

In my ideal world, *that's* how this conversation would start.

Then we'd spend a leisurely afternoon talking about our joys, sorrows, hopes, dreams, and *especially* our friend Jesus. We'd share like fearless five-year-olds, laughing, crying, then laughing again, without a single worry about how long we'd been there or how many calories we'd consumed.

This book is my invitation to coffee: *four coffee dates, in fact.*

Each *Coffee Chat* is designed to last about as long as one leisurely coffee date, and is divided up into chapters (or *"sips"*) in case you don't have time to read a whole *Coffee Chat* in one sitting. I hope this will give us a chance to slow down and share some meaningful moments together.

Here's what we'll talk about in our four conversations...

MY STORY	How I "stumbled" into coffee-date discipling
YOUR STORY	Have you ever considered making disciples yourself?
HER STORY	*Relational tools* for helping a friend build her life on Jesus
GOD'S STORY	*Mentoring milestones* to help her live out her God-story

I hope that all four *Coffee Chats* will inspire and equip you to drink more deeply of Christ than ever before—and to pour into others as freely as He's poured into you.

Yet I'll tell you straight out: *I'm NOT the cup-filler.* As I mentioned before, only the Father, Son, and Holy Spirit can fill our cups with the refreshing blend of truth and love we so desperately need. Our part is to simply ask, receive, and pass it on.

So find yourself a cozy spot and let's drink in God's goodness together, one delicious life-giving sip at a time!

SIP 1

ACCIDENTALLY
ON PURPOSE

I don't know if we each have a destiny,
or if we're all just floating around
accidental-like on a breeze.
But I think maybe it's both.
Maybe both are happening at the same time.
FORREST GUMP

What men call accident is God's own part.
PHILIP JAMES BAILEY

I never started out to be a discipler—I just stumbled into it.

At least that's how it looked to me at the time.

About a dozen years ago, my husband and I attended a weekend seminar on spiritual gifts. Even though I'd been a believer since childhood, had hungrily devoured every "deeper life" teaching I ever encountered, and even spent several years in full-time ministry, this was still my first exposure to a "find your spiritual gifts" class. I soaked it in like a sponge.

As a follow-up to the seminar, each participant was invited to meet with the leaders to help clarify their spiritual gifts and discover where they could best serve in the church. When my turn came, all I could think was, *Please, oh please, oh please! How can I join the team that meets with people?* That sounded like heaven to me.

To my delight, God opened the door for me to do just that, and a few weeks later I met with my first "gift-seeking" participants.

Almost all of them were new believers who were still learning the basics of the faith. Some of them had spiritual gifts like teaching or leadership, which (it seemed to me) required a bit of experience and maturity to use wisely. I remember thinking, *I'm no expert, but don't these people need a little more instruction before we unleash them on the body of Christ?*

One of the new believers was a young woman in her twenties. She was sweet, vivacious, and eager to learn. She and I chatted easily about various subjects and there seemed to be a genuine rapport developing between us. Halfway through our time together, I found myself wishing I knew someone who could walk her through the first few steps of her new life with Jesus.

As we talked, a strange thing happened. The word *discipleship* kept flashing through my mind—a word that was definitely not part of my daily vocabulary. I wasn't quite sure what to make of it. Then toward the end of our session, I suddenly heard myself say, "You know, before you dive into serving, you might wanna consider getting discipled first."

Like I even knew what that was, right?

Yet spurred on by a faint mental image of the Apostle Paul and Timothy huddled over a scroll, I added, "That's when you meet with a more experienced believer who helps you get more established in your faith. Is that something you'd be interested in?"

I felt like Wile E. Coyote who'd just run off a cliff—cuz if she said yes, I'd better learn to fly reeeeeeeal quick.

With nothing but air beneath my feet, I kept going.

"You know, I've never actually discipled anyone myself, but if you're game...I'd be willing to give it a try. Why don't we both pray about it this week?"

She nodded and smiled.

I gulped and prayed.

And hoped against hope I wouldn't hit the ground with a deafening splat.

Yet I also felt a rising sense of anticipation—and a thrill of excitement the following week when we both heard "yes" from God. So *accidentally on purpose,* the die was cast.

Suddenly I was a discipler.

SIP 2

FROM ACCIDENTAL
TO INTENTIONAL

Faith is taking the first step,
even when you don't see the whole staircase.
MARTIN LUTHER KING, JR.

Love is our true destiny.
We do not find the meaning of life by ourselves alone—
we find it with another.
THOMAS MERTON

Like I said, I sort of stumbled my way into this whole discipling thing by accident. At least that's how it looked from *my* side of the coin. On the flip side, it's fairly clear that God had it planned from the moment He thought me up.

I just had to live my way into it—and so will you.

Once the girl said yes to me discipling her, a deep sense of peace told me God was leading. *Yet I had no idea what to do next.* So with hope in my heart, I made a beeline for the Christian bookstore. I figured they had to have some kind of beginners' Bible study I could use to get started.

The pickings were slim, but I finally found a study that was based on Scripture, written for new believers, and lasted six weeks. That was good enough for me.

We started meeting weekly at the church office in an open-air conference room, and soon we were working our way through the study. Our personalities were a good fit and I enjoyed hearing about her life and studying the Bible side by side. Soon we settled into a comfortable rhythm, and I gradually began to recognize God's still small voice leading and guiding our times together.

One day as I was tidying up the conference room, the assistant pastor's wife came walking down the stairs from her loft office overhead where (unbeknownst to me) she'd been within earshot of our whole two-hour meeting.

She smiled sweetly and said, "Hey, I think it's going pretty well, don't you?"

My knees almost buckled and I remember thinking: *You'd certainly know better than me—I'm new!*

What followed was a gift-from-God conversation with one of the loveliest women I've ever had the privilege of knowing. The crazy thing was, I'd had a secret wish to get to know her better for quite a while. As my husband once observed, Priscilla was the heart and soul of that church. Love bubbled out of her like water from a spring and we all loved her back with childlike enthusiasm.

In fact, I wouldn't be surprised if at some point everyone who knew her thought they were her favorite, because the truth is, that's how her love made you feel. She was and is a treasure, one of those rare people who radiates the life of Christ to everyone she meets.

Yet before that day, I'd never dreamed of getting to know Priscilla personally. Quite frankly, there were waaaaaayy too many people in line ahead of me! Or so I thought. Nonetheless, our "chance" encounter eventually led to the not-so-accidental blessing God intended all along.

After our stairway chat we agreed to meet again to get better acquainted. As we dialogued back and forth, Priscilla shared some things God had recently been impressing on her heart. Apparently, this was my moment to hear them too, because they've been deeply etched into my spiritual DNA ever since.

For the previous few weeks, Priscilla hadn't been able to stop thinking about Jesus' final words on earth before He ascended to heaven. I remember her nodding her head and saying, "He just won't let me move on from Matthew 28." The longer she pondered, the more clearly she heard the voice of the Holy Spirit say, *Whatever else you do in life, whether you're in full-time ministry or not, you are to personally invest the gospel in women's lives.* Discipleship was to be the default, not the exception. In season and out, for as long as she lived, period.

When she said this, something deep inside me shifted, like a GPS rerouting to a new destination or a sunflower turning its face toward the sun. Here are Jesus' words that rocked both our worlds.

Go and make disciples of all nations, baptizing them in the name of the Father and of the Son and of the Holy Spirit, and teaching them to obey everything I have commanded you.

MATTHEW 28:18-20

This was to be our ground zero—our "new normal" as followers of Jesus.

Go and make disciples.

These words were not unfamiliar to me. I'd heard them mentioned in teachings and sermons for years, yet I'd never heard anyone talk about them the way Priscilla did. There was a sense of holy awe in her voice, as if Jesus had spoken them to her that very morning over coffee: *a lifestyle of discipleship.*

As Priscilla spoke, a fire was kindled in my heart that has been inextinguishable ever since. For the first time in my life I understood that the essential calling of *every* believer is to make disciples. It's how we're meant to "do life" in the kingdom of God.

In a moment it all was so clear. I couldn't believe I'd never seen it before. Yet I didn't sense the Lord rolling His eyes or condemning me in any way. Apparently, this was my God-ordained moment to grasp the wonder of His plan—and step out in faith.

In that moment I knew I was *born* for this.

And so were you.

SIP 3

WATCHING GOD FILL THE MENTOR GAP

The moment one commits oneself,
then providence moves too.
W. H. MURRAY

Leap and the net will appear.
JOHN BURROUGHS

When I first started on the road to making disciples, I didn't have a map to follow. All I knew was: *Jesus had disciples, and He'd given them instructions to go and make more.* Yet as to how they actually did it, I was mostly guessing.

The main reason for this lack of information was the fact that I'd never been discipled myself. Come to think of it, neither had any of my friends. I suppose we understood the concept in a "that's how the early church did it" sort of way, but none of us had ever experienced it firsthand.

Maybe the same is true for you.

But take heart, the Holy Spirit is more than able to fill your mentor gap!

In my case, what started as lack of experience turned out to be downright exhilarating in the long run—because my lack of experience forced me to rely on God for guidance. It also compelled me to take steps of faith, which caused me to grow by leaps and bounds.

And one of those leaps led me to Priscilla.

Shortly after she shared about The Great Commission I thought, *Wouldn't it be amazing if Priscilla could disciple me—you know, retroactively?* Yet I couldn't bring myself to admit it out loud. After all, she was a very sought-after lady.

There's no way she'd ever have time for me, I told myself.

Soon all sorts of other voices joined in. *Who do you think you are? There are plenty of other people she'd rather mentor than you. Besides, think how awful you'd feel if you asked and she said no!* And on and on it went.

Meanwhile, to my surprise, Priscilla and I ended up having another informal conversation or two about our new favorite subject: **spiritual**

mentoring. She encouraged my fledgling efforts and told me about the lady who had invested in her years earlier. These encounters only intensified my longing to ask her to do the same for me.

But my lips were sealed.

Then one day I found my courage. Like a scared kid on Santa's lap, I blurted out my request. "You know, I was wondering, would you ever consider...discipling me? I know I've already been a believer a long time...but what I *really* feel the need for is the *relational* part. You know, having an older woman...not that you're all *that* much older...that is, having someone wiser and more experienced who'd actually take the time to get to know me and help me grow...you know, kinda like a spiritual mom. What do you think?"

(awkward pause)

To this day Priscilla's exact response eludes me.

I think she said something about needing to pray about it. I'm sure I did my best to act like it was no big deal, even though it meant the world to me.

But the kindness in her eyes gave me courage.

I told myself, *Even if she says no, at least I finally admitted what I truly want.*

To my utter amazement—a few days later she said yes.

I felt like I'd won the lottery.

For the next year, I had the privilege of meeting with this incredible woman on a weekly basis. I got to experience firsthand what it's like to have another believer invest in you spiritually.

In a word, it was life-changing.

Yet the truth is, being discipled didn't change Jesus' love for me one iota. It simply made His love more *tangible* for my flesh-and-blood heart to grasp. Who knows, maybe that's a big part of why He commanded us to disciple each other in the first place? To help us better internalize the love and truth He's already given us.

In my case, I felt as if I'd been emotionally un-freeze-tagged for the first time in my life. I think deep down I'd been waiting for decades to feel truly "seen" by someone. Even though I'd been learning and growing and following Jesus for years, there was a huge part of my heart that could only be healed through deeper connection with His people, up close and personal.

Over time, Priscilla became a dear and trusted friend.

She listened, laughed, cried, and prayed. She learned how I was wired, and reflected to me the strengths she saw. She covered my weaknesses and graciously bathed them in prayer. She rejoiced when I rejoiced and wept when I wept. When I succeeded, she was so happy you'd have thought the victory was her own. When my heart grew faint, she empathized and cheered me on.

I can still hear her sweet voice reminding me "the gifts and callings of God are irrevocable" and encouraging me to develop "a tough mind and a tender heart." She was also transparent about her own weaknesses in a way that allowed the life of Christ to shine through her even more brightly. Whether she was listening, loving, encouraging, sharing, or simply calling me "kiddo," I could always see the heart of Jesus in her eyes.

There's something incredibly powerful about meeting with another believer eyeball to eyeball, week in and week out. They get to know your strengths, weaknesses, joys, sorrows, and the ebb and flow of the way you "do life." They learn the kinds of things that encourage you, and the kinds of things that trip you up. Their very presence in your life enables you to grow, process, heal, discover, risk, and change into the image of Jesus much more quickly and thoroughly than you ever dreamed possible.

Of course, Jesus Himself had *already* been my Discipler for years, and no human relationship could ever compare to Him. Yet the year with Priscilla helped deepen and intensify my relationship with Jesus like never before.

I also had the privilege of helping her start a discipleship ministry at our church. She undertook the herculean task of simultaneously discipling eight or nine women who were interested in learning to disciple others. I'm still not sure how she managed it.

Priscilla also planted in my heart the ideas of **multiplication** and **spiritual legacy**. Through looking over her shoulder, I got a glimpse of how discipleship can spread from person to person and become a way of life. I also came to realize that every woman I would ever disciple would be the spiritual grandchild of this precious woman who God brought into my life.

These days we live thousands of miles apart, yet whenever we do connect it feels like coming home. To this day, Priscilla consistently reminds me of who I am in Christ and cheers me on in my efforts for the kingdom. Our deep love for each other (and our mutual love for Jesus and "His girls") continues to be an ongoing source of encouragement and joy.

A PATCHWORK OF MENTORS

Since my time with Priscilla, God has graciously continued to fill my mentor gap in specific seasons of need. Now and then He surprises me with yet another more-experienced disciple who walks with me for this or that leg of the journey. Some of them have served as *official* mentors, while others have loved and supported me in more informal *as-you-go* ways. Yet *each* of them has made an incredible impact on my life.

I'd love to briefly share their stories...

- **To introduce you** to my beloved mentors
- **To spur memories** of those who've invested in *your* life
- **To provide examples** of mentoring styles to choose from
- **To nurture hope** in those still longing for a spiritual mentor

Consistent Big Sis (Maryann)

I first met Maryann when we both worked part-time at a local Christian bookstore. She was in her mid-thirties and highly educated. I was a college freshman with an undeclared major. On paper our **friendship** didn't add up, yet heart-wise we always clicked. I spent a lot of time at Maryann's apartment—talking, praying, and just hanging out. As single girls on a budget, we shared dinners of tuna, cottage cheese, and wheat thins so often that to this day neither of us can eat those foods without thinking of the other.

Maryann never talked down to me. Instead, she shared her day-to-day challenges and listened to mine as if both sides of the conversation were of equal value. Though I didn't have language for it at the time, I now understand that my "big sis" modeled **godly love** and **acceptance** long before I had the ability to love or accept myself. She encouraged me in my faith and treated me with such **dignity** that I always felt a little taller in her presence.

Maryann continues to be a river of blessing to me and countless others, even now as she bravely battles ovarian cancer. In a season when most would shift their focus inward, her lifelong habit of loving the person in front of her has turned her cancer journey into a mission field. Regardless of how God completes her earthly story, Maryann's life will bear fruit for all eternity.

As-You-Go Nurturer (Beth)

Another woman who made a powerful impact on my life is a gentle-hearted woman named Beth. She's one of those salt-of-the-earth types who never makes a fuss about herself, yet always manages to add dignity and grace to the lives of those around her.

In my twenties and thirties, I dealt with increasingly intense depression. By the time I started working in an office with Beth, the despair was so thick I could barely function. I felt lost, confused, and deep-down ineligible for everything that truly mattered to me. Every day was an excruciating struggle, like dragging a thousand-ton boulder up the side of Mt. Everest. This went on for one of the longest years of my entire life. I would have been utterly hopeless except for one thing: *Beth.*

We worked in the same office and every day she was there, **accepting, loving, including, honoring,** and **listening,** when I had nothing to give her in return. She kept me close to her heart and made it look as effortless as breathing. *Wherever she went, she took me along with her.* All I had the strength to do was drink it in and love her back. Yet as I did, I slowly gained the courage to keep living another day—and another and another.

I wish I could tell you Beth's lavish investment of love instantly cured my depression—yet as it turned out, she was only part of my healing. It would take an aborted suicide attempt a year later to finally scare me enough to get medical help for my depression. That in turn led to in-depth Christian counseling, learning to renew my mind in Scripture—and as they say, the rest is history.

Yet without Beth's daily doses of love way back when, it's entirely possible I might've been overcome by despair and entirely missed the joy, purpose, and abiding Presence of God that fill my life today.

Primary Discipler (Priscilla)

You've already heard the wonderful story of how I met this precious lady. Since Priscilla was my first official mentor, she of course holds a special place in my heart.

She gave me the gifts of **affirmation** and **attention** and to this day reminds me of who I am whenever we speak. She also gave me the gifts of **loving nurture, godly vision,** and **equipping** for making disciples.

Loving Launcher (Paula)

I met this wise and witty pastor's wife at a speaker's conference when I first began writing and speaking. Even though Paula and I lived in different states, she made time to hear my heart, listen to my dreams, and eventually blew my mind by declaring, "I believe God wants me to help you get started."

Over the next couple years, Paula put her faith into action by giving me various opportunities to do comedy, lead worship, or speak at events she hosted—without having seen me do so beforehand! As if that weren't enough, she also invited me to co-write her autobiography, *The Pastor Driven Wife.* I'm forever grateful to Paula for taking the time to invest in me, and to this day I credit her love-in-action mentoring style for giving me the much-needed gifts of **noticing, nudging, experience,** and **godly confidence**.

A lady from her church once told me, "Paula sees a diamond in every rock." I'm very grateful to be one of the "rocks" Paula saw. I'm keenly aware that whatever books I write or lives I'm able to touch, I owe a huge debt of gratitude to Paula for taking the time to invest herself in a future only eyes of faith could see.

Mutual Encourager (Barb)

A year or so later, God brought another as-you-go mentor into my life. Her name was Barb and on the surface we didn't have much in common. She was a grandma and Bible teacher with a slightly reserved style, while I was a quirky, animated mid-lifer—yet right away we both sensed something "there" between us. What followed was a year or two of weekly talk-til-you-drop lunches where we each poured out our respective joys, sorrows, and random thoughts without reserve—and then prayed over them together. We also served as each other's creative sounding board. She read aloud the rough draft of her weekly Bible study, while I regaled her with stories of whatever creative ministry project I was working on at the time.

I always left Barb's presence feeling loved, valued, and reassured that God was indeed building good things into my life—even if they looked a bit messy at the moment. During a season when I was taking all kinds of creative risks, Barb gave me the gifts of **stability, safety, paying attention, processing,** and **prayerful support**.

More than once I considered asking her to officially mentor me, yet somehow the question never felt quite right. In a way, it feels like we kind of mutually mentored each other—I stretched her and she stabilized me. Yet I always knew Barb's investment of time and energy in me was nurturing, motherly, and intentional. She could have kept our friendship at a distance, but instead she embraced it wholeheartedly and made room for me in her life with a tenderness one usually reserves for family. Barb's love and attention made a huge difference in my life, and I honor her to this day as one of my beloved mentors.

Unbridled Enthusiast (Margie)

When I first began writing this book, I did so with intense passion and great joy. Yet as the writing process progressed, I felt more and more isolated. Writing can be a lonely venture, and not everyone understands what it's like to face the blank page, day in and day out, with the constant pressure to write down words that mirror what God's put on your heart.

After several weeks of struggle, it finally dawned on me: *I need another mentor to help me finish the book on spiritual mentoring!* Yet as it happened, none of my previous mentors were available. *Besides,* I thought, *haven't you already had more than your share?*

Still the longing intensified. Almost to the boiling point, I broke down and asked God directly.

Red-faced and snotty-nosed, I ugly cried my way through the whole dramatic outburst, which sounded more like a distraught child's wail than it did a prayer. Afterwards I felt calm and at peace, confident that whatever God answered, I could live with.

I also sent a quick text to a couple women, asking if they had a moment to pray over the phone. One of them was a lady named Margie who I'd met at a conference a year or so earlier.

Suffice to say, I've never met anyone quite like Margie.

Her unique brand of hurricane-force exhortation was down-to-your-toes energizing and sweetly encouraging all rolled into one. Praying with Margie was like plugging your heart into triple-strength Holy Spirit amperage, almost to the point of blowing your circuits—yet I always walked away feeling more loved, refreshed, and energized to serve God than I ever imagined was possible.

Plus, you know that connected feeling you get when someone gives you their full attention?

Oh, how I hope you do.

There's nothing quite so affirming as having someone deep down listen to you—*not just to what you say, but to who you are*—and truly invest themselves in what they hear. That's how it was talking with Margie. We both felt a strong sense of destiny about that first conversation, as if we'd stumbled onto a priceless treasure God had intentionally placed in our path.

As I wrote the first draft of this book, Margie continued to cheer me on as a friend, fellow writer, and spiritual "mother in the house." God gifted her with such a supernatural enthusiasm for me (and for those who would read this book) that sometimes it even blew *her* circuits!

Whenever I needed to be reminded of who I was, or the glorious privilege of what God had called me to do, I called Margie. Talking with her brought a fresh infusion of confidence and contagious enthusiasm for all things God-ward. After each conversation, I hung up the phone feeling grateful to be "a daughter of the Most High God," who had so graciously sent Mama Margie my way when I needed her most.

She gave me the gifts of **listening, godly enthusiasm, prophetic prayer, vision,** and **confidence**.

Then out of nowhere, a month before the first draft was finished, I received a five-word text from a mutual friend that rocked my world: "Our precious Margie is gone."

My brain couldn't process the words.

Gone where?!

After a few minutes of frantic online investigation, the unthinkable was confirmed. Earlier that day Margie had been involved in a head-on collision—and a short time later she crossed over into heaven. Suddenly the whole universe seemed cold and distant.

I'd never known anyone quite as alive as Margie. It seemed inconceivable that someone so vibrant could be taken so quickly, and the thought of never speaking with her again this side of heaven seemed unbearable.

I threw myself on the floor and wailed, "Please Lord, no! Not Margie! I can't finish the book without Margie!" In the silence that followed, I heard her voice in my head say clear as a bell: *Now that is ridiculous. Of course you can do it—you've got Jesus!*

Suddenly I burst out laughing. Right there on the bathroom floor, with freshly-cried tears still streaming down my face. Because, of course, she was right—Jesus and I *could* do it without her.

(and you reading this chapter is living proof...)

Yet sometimes my heart still aches for Mama Margie. At the end of my life, I can't wait to hear her spunky little voice cheering me across the finish line as she points me toward the waiting arms of Jesus.

We have a lot to catch up on.

And she'll *definitely* want to hear about you.

GOD'S GOT YOU COVERED

By now you may be thinking, *Okay, fine, I get it. You've had tons of great mentors, hooray for you. But just so you know, most of us haven't been that lucky.*

Believe me, I get it.

Because despite how it sounds, I lived long decades of my life without mentoring of any kind. In fact, that's a big part of what led to my depression—feeling so deeply unknown and un-invested in that I misinterpreted it as God's disinterest in me, to the point of utter despair.

If you're feeling anything remotely similar, *please know my heart is right there with you.* In fact, while writing this chapter I found myself pleading with you.

Please-oh-please don't lose heart and stop reading. Don't believe the lie that all this is great, but none of it's for you. I know how it feels to wonder if your turn will EVER come. I know all these stories sound too good to be true. Yet I also know what it's like to watch God come through for you in incredible ways when you LEAST expect it.

So, with all my heart I'm here to say...

Beloved girl,
God has not forgotten you.

He has thoroughly and absolutely
Got. You. Covered.

He may bring you a primary discipler like Priscilla or a loving launcher like Paula. A big sister like Maryann or a mutual encourager like Barb. An as-you-go nurturer like Beth or an unbridled enthusiast like Margie.

Or at times, He may lead you through a privileged season *with Him and Him alone as your Beloved Discipler*, learning lessons of intimate trust that are best developed in deep solitude with Him.

Yet whatever option He chooses for you in any given season, it's always out of *love* for you that He chooses. And *loving obedience* enables you to walk through each new door God brings your way.

So when He tells you to step out in faith—*gather up your courage and go for it!* Then watch in amazement as Christ Himself steps in to fill your mentor gap.

Not just to a quarter or half tank—*but to overflowing*.

SIP 4

LEARNING TO FOSTER A FUTON FAMILY

You have not chosen one another,
but I have chosen you for one another.
C.S. LEWIS

God places the lonely in families;
he sets the prisoners free and gives them joy.
PSALM 68:6 (NLT)

I once overheard someone say: "When we look into the future, all we see are man's subjective choices. Yet when we look into the past, all we see is the sovereignty of God."

Over the past several years I've been privileged to get to know some amazing young women, meeting with them in coffeeshops, restaurants, or on the "discipleship futon" in my home. I never could've engineered these connections—but I'm so glad God in His sovereignty did.

If a picture is worth a thousand words, then a story is worth a gazillion. This chapter contains a few stories from my own experience as a spiritual mentor. I chose these examples because each one approaches the process from a slightly different angle, according to the personality and circumstances of the person involved. Each of these young women logged a significant amount of "futon time" and is now part of my irreplaceable futon family.

Teachable Heart (Jaimee)

ALDOUS HUXLEY - *Experience teaches only the teachable.*

Sometimes you have a strong feeling God is stirring up a discipleship relationship with someone long before it occurs. That was the case with Jaimee, a beautiful girl in her twenties who looked and sounded for all the world like a real-life Disney princess!

We met as volunteer counselors for a church-sponsored foster camp. She had a heart of gold and was deeply devoted to serving the kids, even when as a first-time counselor she was assigned to the most challenging and verbally abusive camper there. While many of us "older and wiser" counselors were wringing our hands over this girl's misadventures, Jaimee would repeatedly find her, reason with her, and bring her back to our cabin with the poise and patience of someone twice her age.

After camp, Jaimee and I ran into each other from time to time, and even talked and prayed together occasionally. Soon I felt that familiar sense that God might be stirring up a mentoring relationship between us. Yet a couple of things concerned me.

First, despite her many amazing qualities, Jaimee could also be a bit flakey. Whenever we talked about getting together for coffee she'd gush, "Oh yes, I'd *love* to!" yet she never quite committed to putting something on the calendar. After a couple years of this, I realized it was pointless to keep inviting her.

Second, during one of our chance conversations she mentioned she'd recently joined a discipleship small group, which was led by our church's women's ministry director. I remember rejoicing with her yet also feeling a faint sense of sadness, because deep down I still sensed God was going to make a way for me to mentor her. I figured I must've misunderstood what the Lord was saying, and chalked it up to experience.

Then one day I got a call from the women's director. She explained Jaimee had been part of her small group for the past few months and that she thought very highly of her. Yet recently she'd begun to wonder if the group setting was the best fit for Jaimee. Long story short, she was calling to ask if I'd consider discipling her.

A few minutes later, Jaimee called me with the same request.

Apparently she had recently reread her old journals and was reminded of how deeply our periodic conversations had impacted her life.

This was two years after I sensed I was going to mentor her!

Yet I still I had one nagging concern.

"Wow Jaimee, that sounds amazing, and I would love to disciple you. Yet I've noticed it's practically impossible to pin you down long enough to even schedule coffee, much less meeting regularly. So honestly, for me to consider discipling you...I'd need you to make it a *top* priority."

Her response made the two years of waiting more than worth it.

"Oh yeah, I'm learning that about myself: *I'm a flake!* God really used the accountability of the small group to show me that. I'm ready to make some changes. I'll definitely commit to meeting regularly!"

And she was true to her word.

Over the next two years, Jaimee made discipleship her top priority. She was an eager student and remembered what she learned better than anyone I'd ever met. As we talked and prayed our way through each area of her life, I found myself laughing out loud from sheer amazement that she could retain so much *and* incorporate the lessons she learned into everyday life. Witnessing her enthusiasm for hearing and obeying God often brought refreshment to my own heart.

I also discovered that whatever Jaimee received would soon get passed on to others. She was very open about her relationship with Jesus, and she had no qualms about sitting her girlfriends down and teaching them something she'd recently learned. I began hearing reports of one friend or another who was interested in being mentored because "I've seen the changes in Jaimee's life." Soon I was investing in a growing circle of girls, formally and informally, because of the "advance work" God was doing through her.

As I got to know her better, I discovered she had a much deeper side than most people ever got to see, and my respect for her grew with each passing week. I also discovered that underneath her Disney princess exterior she was wonderfully quirky and down-to-earth. Or as I often told her, "Girl, you're my same brand o' goober!"

Oh, how we loved getting to know God better together as we laughed and cried our way through dozens of "futon Friday" afternoons. I'll never forget her sweet face, exuberant laugh, or the childlike way she'd rest her head on my shoulder now and then when her heart was especially sad or happy.

In recent years, she's gone through challenging circumstances of all shapes and sizes. And through it all, *the anchor holds.* Jesus has never released His grip on her hand, and she continues to allow Him to teach her and secure her through good times and bad.

Now and then she calls me up just to say, "I got out my journal today and started refreshing those habits you taught me!"

That's music to a spiritual mama's ears.

I love that *review, follow-through,* and *new growth* have become a regular habit for this dedicated wife, mother, and professional who is now the *opposite* of flakey.

Though Jaimee has parents of her own who love her dearly, and who I could never replace, I still dare to think of her as my beloved spiritual daughter and her family as an extension of our own. I can't wait to see what God has in store for this treasure of a girl who's stolen her way into my heart in such a special way.

Through her I've seen firsthand how He weaves the hearts of His children together so intricately, there's no turning back.

As for me—*I'd never want to!*

Preparing The Bride (Micah)

REV. 21:2 *(ESV)* - *Prepared as a bride adorned for her husband.*

I met Micah through yet another "chance" encounter at a new members' gathering at our church. As we went around the circle to introduce ourselves, Micah and her dad were introduced together. I remember thinking, "Wow, that man has a *really* young wife!" A moment's conversation soon corrected my error. But part of what made it seem plausible was a certain air of maturity about Micah that exceeded her years.

As we continued to get acquainted, I mentioned I was starting a small group at my house for young women in their twenties. Micah immediately warmed to the idea, so we exchanged contact information.

A short while later, our small group began. And I do mean *small*. There was me, one other girl, and Micah. Even so, our first meeting went well and both girls seemed enthusiastic, yet Micah didn't say a whole lot. The next week the other girl had a schedule conflict, so it was just me and Micah. What a stunning difference with just the two of us! Conversation flowed far more easily for Micah, and as her gentle-spirited personality rose to the surface, I discovered she was also quite funny and insightful.

The next week, the other girl realized she had an ongoing schedule conflict. But since Micah and I already had it on our calendars, we decided to keep meeting. What a blessing that "small" decision turned out to be.

Micah's way of looking at things was refreshingly simple, and I sensed God's delight in her welling up in my own heart as she shared each week. It was like watching a time-lapse video of a flower opening, one gentle, exquisite petal at a time. Come to think of it, a flower is the perfect metaphor for Micah, since at age twenty-one she already considered herself a late bloomer.

She'd always envisioned going to college, yet when all her friends headed off to university right after high school, she found herself hanging back. She wasn't quite sure what major to choose, so she decided to work for a while until she figured things out. Yet as one year turned into two, and now was pushing three, she still didn't feel any clearer on God's specific direction for her life.

At her age, I had experienced a similar challenge. Although I had a huge desire to make a difference in the world, my own "type B" temperament often held me back.

So one night during our mentoring meeting, I had an idea. I asked, "Micah, are you willing to try an exercise with me?" She nodded yes. I gave her some blank paper and grabbed the egg timer from the kitchen.

"Okay, I'm gonna ask you some questions and I want you to answer them super quickly—probably more quickly than you're comfortable with. But I'm hopeful the speed will spur you on to answer more from your gut than from your head."

I set the timer, prayed for wisdom, and started firing questions at her.

What group of people do you feel most passionate about helping? What are three areas of ministry you'd love to explore if you had the courage? What's a next step you could take to explore each of those areas?

I half expected Micah to balk, but by the time the timer rang she had a page full of answers. With each one she read aloud, her voice grew stronger. With each action step she listed, her demeanor changed and her eyes began to sparkle. We'd stumbled onto something that worked! Of course, in hindsight I realized God had probably been leading up to this moment for months.

After that night, Micah reported in each week on her action steps, roadblocks, and victories. She had a heart to work with inner city children, so she signed up for a mission trip to Hong Kong. She enjoyed working with graphic design, so she investigated a school or two in the area. Slowly but surely, God was revealing Micah to herself.

Months later I was asked to co-lead a new group at our church for women in their twenties. I asked Micah if she'd like to join the group and she said yes. It was an exciting time. Four leaders. Twenty-five girls. And one incredible Holy Spirit moving among us—molding, shaping, bonding us together, and teaching each one to hear His voice more clearly.

About a year later, though I'd fallen head over heels in love with that group of girls, I realized my season of group ministry was drawing to a close. I always knew my sweet spot was primarily one-on-one mentoring, and I was already feeling drawn to set aside time to write this book. After I stopped attending the group meetings, Micah and I fell out of touch for a while. A few months later, we finally managed to squeeze in a lunch date and settled down for some serious catching up.

"So Micah, what've you been up to?"

"Well—I just got engaged."

I was floored. In all the time we'd spent together, dating and marriage hadn't even made an appearance on Micah's here-and-now radar! Plus, I'd seen quite a few passionate God-seekers make a sudden screeching U-turn when the "perfect guy" suddenly appeared on the horizon.

To put it mildly, I was skeptical.

Yet as Micah began telling me about her fiancé, my mind and heart were quickly put at ease.

First, she'd known him longer than I imagined. Second, he was a believer. And third, it sounded as if they had focused on getting to know each other, warts and all. The more I heard, the better I felt.

They were deeply in love, yet they also seemed to be making eyes-wide-open choices about their own strengths and weaknesses, based on something deeper than feelings. They'd even had their first argument and lived to tell the tale, and I could already see the give-and-take relational patterns of a healthy marriage starting to develop.

By the time I walked to my car after lunch, I could breathe freely again. I even found myself doing a little "happy dance" on their behalf.

When the wedding day arrived a few months later, I couldn't wait to see Micah and Bill tie the knot. It was a simple yet beautiful ceremony (just like Micah), and though I was no relation to anyone there, I felt like a proud mama waiting for her girl to walk down the aisle.

As Micah and her father entered the church, I caught my breath. She was stunning! *The kind of beauty reserved for mythical queens in fairy tales.* Not only that, but her poise and grace were riveting. Every gesture of her hand, every glance of her eye, made me want to weep for joy.

As she and Bill stood at the altar, I realized she was truly a woman now. I was humbled to have played a small part in her coming of age, and found myself rejoicing over her like the daughters of Jerusalem must've rejoiced over Solomon's bride in the Song of Songs.

I didn't plan to stay long at the reception. I only intended to give the bride and groom a quick hug, snap a picture, and be on my way. But God had other plans. As she and Bill walked through the entryway, Micah suddenly headed straight for me. Everyone was eager for them to keep moving, yet Micah seemed oblivious. She stopped, gave me a hug, chatted casually, posed for a cozy picture, and hugged me some more. *The whole world seemed to freeze in place as we savored our special moment.*

On the way home, I marveled at how beautiful Micah looked, how enraptured her groom had been, and the queenly grace that flowed from her every glance and gesture. Suddenly I recognized in hindsight what I'd missed in the moment.

Unbeknownst to Micah, and to me, God had been using our time together to refine, beautify, and prepare her heart for life with her husband, much like Queen Esther preparing herself to be presented to the king.

The moment had come—the bride was ready.

Let the wedding feast begin!

Gentle Strengthener (Gwyn)

PROVERBS 31:10-12 (ESV) - *An excellent wife, who can find? She is far more precious than jewels. The heart of her husband trusts in her, and he will have no lack of gain. She does him good, and not harm, all the days of her life.*

When I met Gwyn, she was a single girl in her early thirties, a beautiful brunette with a warm smile and a welcoming personality. We sat at the same table at a church event and struck up a conversation almost immediately. Gwyn clearly had a heart for God, and there was a special sweetness to our interaction that got my attention.

After a few minutes I found myself wondering, *Lord is there something more going on here?* But "hey, I wonder if I'm supposed to disciple you" isn't the sort of thing you blurt out mid-conversation when you've just met someone. So, as God has taught me to do over the years, I tucked those thoughts away, trusting that if they truly were from Him, He'd make it clear when the time was right.

That same day, Gwyn met another lady at our table named Luci who had a son about her age. Soon Gwyn and Luci were deeply engrossed in conversation and I decided to bow out and let them get acquainted. A few months later, I bumped into Gwyn at church and she mentioned that Luci had started mentoring her.

To be honest, I was kinda surprised that God had led someone else to mentor her, because once I got that, *Hmmm, what are you up to, Lord?* feeling about someone, it usually led to something deeper. I reminded myself that God was free to work through anyone He wanted, and once again wondered if maybe I'd made a mistake. Meanwhile Gwyn and I continued to be casual friends and saw each other at church from time to time.

A year or so later, I heard Gwyn was engaged to Luci's son Randy!

Shortly after their wedding, I met Randy for the first time. He was a handsome, sweet-spirited young man and it was easy to see why Gwyn had fallen in love with him. As we said our goodbyes, she pulled me aside and said, "A while back you mentioned that you do mentoring, and I wondered...would you consider mentoring me as I start my marriage?"

She went on to explain what a huge blessing Luci had been to her, yet she sensed it might be time for a change, now that her mentor had become her mother-in-law. We both agreed to pray about it, and after a week or so we both felt like the answer was yes.

Once again, God had confirmed His gentle nudge in my heart from nearly two years earlier. I never could have envisioned the perfectly timed relationships that unfolded between Gwyn and Luci, Gwyn and Randy, and eventually Gwyn and myself. But God knew all along.

As a rule, my first mentoring meeting with someone is fairly low key. We have coffee, get acquainted, discuss how the process works, and set one small goal, maybe two. But there was nothing "usual" about this night.

When I opened the front door, Gwyn was visibly upset. Before we even got to the futon, she was in tears. "Oh Kim, I'm pregnant!" she cried. At this point she and Randy had been married just over a month and never in their wildest dreams had they anticipated starting a family this soon after the wedding. Like an overwhelmed child, she fell into my arms as a flood of tears spilled out. Once she calmed down, her countenance changed and a look of strength returned to her deep brown eyes.

"Of course, I'm thrilled to have a new life growing inside me—what an honor to be someone's mother! It's just that everything happened so fast, and so unexpectedly—well, it hit me pretty hard."

They'd gone from newly married to new parents in the space of a heartbeat, which meant their expected season of "just the two of us" had disappeared just as quickly. Yet as the shock began to wear off, she realized this new season they were entering was equally precious. God was giving her and Randy a whole new set of challenges—and delights— to prepare for.

That first night, I asked Gwyn to pray about what she wanted to focus on in our time together. Since so much of the baby prep would have built-in prompts—doctor visits, baby showers, and such—she was concerned that her relationship with Randy might suffer. So Gwyn decided she wanted to focus on learning to be a good wife. After talking it over, we decided to study Proverbs 31.

Week by week we each read and studied a group of verses on our own, and then compared notes once we met together. It was a rich time of learning for both of us. We each saw areas where we could learn and grow, and it was inspiring for me to witness Gwyn's tender heart toward her husband. Naturally they went through their share of newlywed growing pains, yet step by step they navigated those challenges together.

I was especially struck by how Gwyn was learning to love the *actual* man God had given her, rather than focusing on *how men are* in general. Randy was a loving, gentle-hearted soul who sometimes struggled with decisiveness. As a young expectant mother, Gwyn longed to feel more financially secure, see him take a stand, and bring up issues they needed to discuss. And at times he absolutely did. Yet when he didn't, it was a real struggle for Gwyn to be patient, trust God, and lean into His wisdom for when to speak and when to remain silent.

So early on, she set her heart on trusting God to work *in and through* Randy's temperament, rather than trying to change him. It was a beautiful thing to watch. Although there were times she wished he would take charge more, she did her best not to shame or disrespect him—reminding herself that his tender heart and nurturing nature were two of the things she loved most about him.

One of my favorite things about meeting with Gwyn was praying with her. She has a way of praying that is incredibly intimate. She doesn't use fancy words or go into detail, yet there's a beautifully childlike quality that draws you in—and how much more must it draw the heart of God. I especially love the way she ends her prayer: "I say these things in Jesus' name." She certainly does.

In the time leading up to her baby's birth, Gwyn and I also talked about concerns she had about becoming a mother. I've heard it said that a baby grows first in a mother's heart, and with Gwyn I got to see this happen up close and personal. It was awe-inspiring to hear her speak of her unborn child with such love and tenderness.

I believe God provided our times together as a "safe harbor" for her during a season of constant change. It was an honor to be able to encourage, nurture, and give momma-bear-hugs to a girl who in a short space of time had become a woman, a wife, and a mother to a newborn child of her own.

These days Gwyn and I keep in touch by text and phone, and we visit her, Randy, and their three kids in California whenever we can. Spending time with this wonderful family is always a highlight, and my husband and I look forward to being part of their lives for many years to come.

Resilient Overcomer (Amy)

C.S. LEWIS - *Though our feelings come and go, God's love for us does not.*

Amy had known the Lord since she was seventeen and had a solid foundation in the basics of the faith. When we met, she was in her thirties and taught at a local high school. With her curly dark hair and bubbly personality, Amy was a delight to be around and probably the last person anyone would expect to struggle with crippling anxiety and depression. In fact, I often told her, "Amy, you're the most cheerful depressed person I've ever met."

While she was originally drawn to discipleship to learn to mentor others, we soon discovered God had deeper things to deal with first. Some devastating events in her preschool years had deeply impacted her ability to process relationships in adulthood.

When she was three years old, Amy's dad kidnapped her to avoid a custody battle with her mom. While her picture wasn't plastered on milk cartons and her father didn't mistreat her in any way, being wrenched away from her mother in such a dramatic fashion still deeply traumatized her little three-year-old heart.

Not only that, but Amy was eventually put in the gut-wrenching position of having to choose between her parents. Devastated and confused, she coped the only way she knew how—*by telling each parent whatever they wanted to hear.* This set in motion a complex pattern of

31

inner shame and conflict that no one could've fully envisioned, and only God Himself could unravel.

Eventually Amy's mom was given full custody and her father was sent to jail, which piled trauma on top of trauma. She later recalled, "I just needed a rock to hold onto in the chaos, but I could never find one."

Once she reached adulthood, Amy's relationship with both parents settled into a more stable pattern, and much of the time her manner was sunny, positive, and optimistic. Yet despite her best efforts to fend them off, periods of deep darkness always returned. In those seasons, she'd experience depression, anxiety attacks, and a harsh inner voice that constantly reminded her she wasn't "doing it right"—especially where trusting God was concerned.

This led to increasingly intense feelings of despair that made it very difficult for Amy to embrace hope. Every time she tried to put her full weight on trusting God, the enemy engulfed her with so much condemnation and outright panic that she quickly retreated in doubt and fear. After many years of this relentless pattern, Amy began to wonder if depression, anxiety, and "not enough" were simply her lot in life.

Although I wasn't trained as a therapist, God made it abundantly clear that He had placed Amy in my life to love and support. For many years, she'd been to counselors and taken meds for depression and anxiety, yet nothing seemed to make a dent in the huge wall of hopelessness and despair that had become her "norm"—plus she hated the side effects. At this point, I figured we had nothing to lose by seeing what God might do through our times together.

For two years we met weekly at my house. Together we brought her feelings into the light, clung to truth, and asked God for breakthrough. When her depression was at its worst, we talked on the phone daily before work, praying and reading our way through the Psalms. When panic attacks hit, she'd call me "mid-attack" for reassuring connection and prayer. Now and then she spent time at our house doing laundry or hanging out, as God bonded our hearts together even further.

To be honest, we didn't always see tangible signs that anything was changing. Yet I strongly sensed that what we were doing was a huge piece of the puzzle. My husband and I were privileged to become a sort of "home base" for Amy's healing, and she has become like family to both of us.

I wish I could report that after those two years, Amy's depression and anxiety magically disappeared. But her battle continued to rage for the next several years. The enemy of her soul stubbornly persisted, and it took years of deep relationship, renewing her mind, and gaining the courage to surrender to God to pry Satan's spindly little fingers off the most vulnerable areas of her heart.

Yet thankfully, over time, her life has made a 180-degree turn toward truth, transformation, and wholeness.

She's learned to connect with God through His Word, journaling prayer, inner healing prayer sessions, and the ebb and flow of everyday life—most of which would have been unthinkable for Amy when we first met. This has led to increased confidence in her ability to hear God's voice and trust His love for her, which has empowered her to release shame and embrace a more courageous way of living.

For one thing, she's not nearly as "nicey-nice" as she used to be. If she has a problem with something (or someone), she's much more likely to speak up for herself and let the chips fall where they may. *This is huge.* She's also taking gradual steps forward in areas such as travel, creativity, and dating—even if those steps don't feel "perfect." *Also huge.*

Each time I talk with Amy, I hear more peace and confidence in her voice. She's moving forward. She's taking risks. She's grieving losses and making room for what's next. Best of all, she's able to put her full weight on her relationship with God, and sounds happier and more hopeful than I've ever heard her.

Now, over a decade later, Amy continues to be one of my favorite people. She's funny, gracious, gritty, and "let's get real" authentic, all rolled into one, and hearing her voice on the phone is enough to make my day. I'm beyond grateful to have this passionate woman of God in my life.

Though we live in different states, we still love to talk and pray together as often as possible. It's an important touch point for both of us, and always spurs us on to greater joy and growth.

For some of us the battle for victory in Christ is more intensely "daily" than for others. *Yet God's promises still hold true.* And Amy has stayed the course like a champion, refusing to give into a way of life or manner of thinking that isn't *all* Jesus died to give her.

A couple of years ago in prayer, I saw this vivid picture of Amy and Jesus walking together along the Sea of Galilee:

He was dressed in white linen and she wore a green velvet gown reminiscent of the queens of Narnia. She was strong and beautiful, with dancing eyes, and her rich dark hair cascaded down her back like a bridal veil.

With the sea on their left and the valley on their right, they strolled along the path in contented silence. Now and then she stopped to gather something—flowers maybe—but the longer I looked, I saw they were actually precious stones: rubies, sapphires, emeralds.

She showed them to Him, one by one, and He responded with smiles and nods. Yet somehow, He didn't seem surprised. Then suddenly I understood. He had hidden these treasures for her Himself, along the very path she'd thought was devoid of hope.

I can't wait to see what God has in store for His beloved Amy girl!

No eye has seen, no ear has heard,
and no mind has imagined
what God has prepared
for those who love him.
2 CORINTHIANS 2:9 (NLT)

Purposeful Ponderer (Alyssa)

ANAIS NIN - *I must be a mermaid, I have no fear of depths, and a great fear of shallow living.*

Now and then you meet someone who genuinely defies description. You can't sum her up with a quick sound bite, and she doesn't fit neatly into clichéd categories. Like an exquisite golden thread woven into a tapestry, she's purely and simply *herself*—and the world is immensely richer for it.

I first met Alyssa at a Bible study for women in their twenties. I was a small group leader and "by chance" she was assigned to my group at the last minute. My first impression was of a slightly disheveled girl with a creative flair who didn't seem all that comfortable in a crowd of strangers. For the life of me, I couldn't tell if she was upset or just extremely introverted.

Either way, I made a mental note to give her time to get her bearings before I called on her. I also found myself praying she wouldn't feel too uncomfortable once I did. So imagine my surprise the first time she opened her mouth.

Words flowed from that girl like a living, breathing sonnet.

Alyssa spoke with a maturity far beyond her years, and her verbal style was an artful blend of intellectual and whimsical. To say I was stunned is an understatement. Once she finished answering the question, she returned to radio silence. Yet by then I was already hooked.

I simply had to get to know this person better!

Week by week, Alyssa grew more comfortable with casual conversation and continued to share when called on during group discussions. And each time she spoke, I felt that same combination of awe and wonder. This girl truly was a treasure.

After the study ended, Alyssa and I decided to meet for lunch to get better acquainted. Meanwhile, I resigned my lay leadership position at the church to start writing this book. When we met a couple weeks later, she brought me up to speed on things in her life and I shared briefly about the book I was writing. She listened politely, yet nothing in her manner gave the impression the topic interested her personally.

So I was quite surprised when toward the end she said, "You know, discipleship is something I'm really sensing a need for in my life. In fact, about a year ago I asked God to bring me a mentor."

I sent up a quick prayer and asked, "So are you saying you're interested in having *me* mentor you?"

To my surprise, she said yes.

I knew in my heart I couldn't say yes without asking the Lord first. He'd long since taught me to give myself a week to pray about it, no matter how sure I felt. Yet this time I needed to check in with Him more than ever, since I was feeling confused about my marching orders.

Lord, didn't You just tell me to go into "book hermit mode"? Do You want me to tackle this huge writing project AND take on a new disciple?

It didn't make sense logically, but deep in my spirit, it did. And after a week of both of us praying, it still did. So we decided to go for it.

Right off the bat, I could tell Alyssa was serious about spiritual growth by the way she made our appointments a priority. She always showed up ready to focus and eager to learn. Each week we talked about the areas God was highlighting in her life, and then worked and prayed our way through them one by one.

For example, as a gifted "right-brainer," speaking in a linear fashion didn't come naturally to her at all—and the verbal disconnect between herself and others left her feeling frustrated. She also had some unresolved issues with her dad that seemed to affect the way she viewed herself. She began to notice these things were getting in the way of her falling more deeply in love with Jesus, because she couldn't seem to let her guard down, even with Him, no matter how hard she tried.

On the face of it, these may not sound much like discipleship issues, but I've discovered that pretty much *anything* in a person's life is a (potential) discipleship issue.

We talked and prayed about these concerns on several occasions, and Alyssa consistently took steps of faith *forward* in response. One week she'd find the courage to dialogue with her dad about something that was bothering her. Another week she'd practice the "right-brain, left-brain" exercises I gave her. Still another, she'd compare her responses and actions to a passage of Scripture she'd read, often without me even suggesting it. As a result, she quickly learned to be a *doer* of the Word rather than just a *hearer*.

Soon, her unique "thought bubble" way of processing life started flowing out in a more poised, linear fashion. She was still very much herself, yet I could tell she felt more and more comfortable being herself in a left-brain world. She also began to exude more confidence and authority in her work, and almost overnight her beauty began to blossom and radiate from deep within.

It was extraordinary to witness.

Around that same time, she also expressed a desire to "ingest the words of Jesus" so we started reading our way through the Gospels. That led to curiosity about Jesus' personality, which led to reading John Eldredge's refreshing book on the subject, *Beautiful Outlaw.*

Shortly afterwards, we tried doing some inductive Bible study together. We bought a gazillion pens and highlighters and worked our way through Jude and Philemon (admittedly the shortest books we could find in the New Testament) til we got the hang of it.

Then Alyssa decided she was ready to go back and study the Gospel of Mark more thoroughly on her own—so she found a Tim Keller book on Mark to study along with it. Soon she was teaching me all she had learned, as I listened in amazement.

In nine short months, Alyssa had gone from introverted right-brainer to confident expounder of the Word!

And the story goes on.

Much like Mary sitting at the feet of Jesus, Alyssa is a natural ponderer. She loves nothing more than to meditate on a thought, idea, visual, or whatever else the Lord brings to mind, and wait to see what He shows her. I love hearing about her most recent musings, and constantly marvel at how much I'm learning in the process.

Watching her bring the various areas of her life to Jesus and surrender them one by one is like watching a work of art being slowly revealed—as bit by bit the Master Sculptor chips away everything that doesn't quite reflect His image.

As I delight in Alyssa's passionate heart, thirst for knowledge, and wonderfully quirky ways, I'm reminded of how full the heart of God must be, overflowing with love for each of His children as if they were the only one.

Because to Him, I believe they are.

And He offers us the privilege of loving them the same way.

One irreplaceable heart at a time.

SIP 5

THERE'S ALWAYS ROOM
FOR ONE MORE

How can there be too many children?
That is like saying there are too many flowers.
MOTHER TERESA

When I first dipped my toe into the discipleship pond, I never envisioned the ripples that would follow.

I had no idea that one disciple would lead to another and another, or that an endless stream of young women would walk their way into my heart, my home, and my life over the next dozen years. And I certainly didn't know that investing in them would lead to discovering my own purpose or daring to write a how-to manual for first-time disciplers.

I just fell in love.

One precious daughter of the King at a time.

And before I knew what hit me, loving and nurturing them had become my heartbeat.

Those of you who are mothers understand this all too well. From the moment you first lay eyes on your newborn child, your heart is captured. To be a mother is "to decide forever to have your heart go walking around outside your body" (Elizabeth Stone). *You could sooner forget to breathe than forget your own child!*

That's how I feel about each girl God has entrusted to my care. Whether He brings her my way for a month, a year, or a lifetime, she becomes a permanent part of my heart, and I'm filled with a sense of holy awe at the privilege of investing in her.

Yet somehow there's always room for "one more."

As one became two, and two became a half dozen, it seemed the most natural thing in the world to invest the gospel in each one's life as best I could. Yet truth be told, it wasn't natural—it was supernatural. God Himself was bringing it about. He was assembling a family for Himself, a futon family of the heart.

Of course I didn't grasp that at first. All I knew was how much I loved the girls He brought my way, and that I was having the time of my life.

I especially enjoyed how they were all so different.

Like a vast field of daisies, they all had similarities, yet no two were identical. One was bubbly and vivacious, while another was deep and thoughtful. One was tough and extroverted, yet another was shy and gentle. There were right-brainers, left-brainers, introverts, extroverts, students, graduates, creatives, professionals, marrieds, singles, blondes, brunettes, and everything else in between.

Each soul was utterly and completely unique.

Yet they all had one thing in common: *They loved Jesus deeply and wanted nothing more than to become His disciple.*

And so the futon family grew. From one, to a handful, to over a decade later when I've almost lost count.

I've met with them for a couple hours each week in every location imaginable: couches, futons, coffeeshops, restaurants, or any quiet place we could grab a hot drink or a hot meal and enjoy some heart-warming conversation about Jesus. We've connected via phone, text, email, Skype, FaceTime, or whatever medium met the need of the moment. I've met with girls locally, state-to-state, and at times even country-to-country.

All it takes is two motivated hearts and the Presence of Jesus—and that can happen just about anywhere.

I usually have about three to six mentoring relationships going at any one time, *officially* discipling about half of them on a regular basis while *as-you-go* investing in the others intermittently as the need arises.

I also find that I'm usually *pre-discipling* someone all the time, since I've learned to pay attention, ask questions, and listen to those God brings across my path. Now and then, I invite everyone over for a girls' night, dinner, or holiday party. This pattern enables me to stay in touch, yet also keep cultivating new relationships—as casual connections often develop into something more intentional over time.

Yet the beauty of discipleship is—there are a zillion ways to do it!

For many, choosing to invest in one new person every one to two years is a great place to start. By making the simple shift from *intending* to *intentional* with even one person, you can make a lasting kingdom impact—without overwhelming your heart or overburdening your schedule. While this may not sound like much at first, do the math.

**If you adopted an "each one reach one" approach,
imagine how many lives you could invest in
during your lifetime!**

You don't have to be Billy Graham to make a kingdom impact. You simply have to *show up* and be *intentional* in your current sphere of influence.

KINGDOM MATH

Plus if you equip those disciples to become disciple *makers*, then we move from simple addition to what I call *kingdom math*. His multiplication versus our simple addition. Because when those we disciple *also* start making disciples, the impact starts exploding exponentially.

Look at these rather stunning statistics.

EVANGELISTIC ADDITION
VS.
DISCIPLEMAKING MULTIPLICATION

YEAR	EVANGELIST	DISCIPLER	D-GROUP OF 4
1	365	2	3
2	730	4	9
3	1,095	8	27
4	1,460	16	81
5	1,825	32	243
6	2,190	64	729
7	2,555	128	2,187
8	2,920	256	6,561
9	3,285	512	19,683
10	3,650	1,024	59,049
11	4,015	2,048	177,147
12	4,380	4,096	531,441
13	4,745	8,192	1,594,323
14	5,110	16,384	4,782,969
15	5,475	32,768	14,348,907
16	5,840	65,536	43,046,721

Note: Reprinted from Robby Gallaty on *Discipleship Multiplication* in D-Groups (*verticallivingministries.com*)

In Genesis, God gave Adam and Eve the command to be fruitful and multiply.

Before He ascended into heaven, Jesus told us to go and make disciples.

**I believe discipleship IS the New Testament
version of "be fruitful and multiply."**

Don't get me wrong, I'm not devaluing parenting. In fact, godly parenting is one of the most crucial, honorable, and *sacrificial* forms of discipleship there is.

You'll find that many of the principles in this book are transferrable to parenting, especially once your kids reach young adulthood. Learning a *coaching* style of mentoring can make all the difference in maintaining a connection with your kids as they make the crucial transition to adulthood. Not only that, but once they're out of the nest you'll *already* be equipped to invest in others beyond your family.

Just as you enjoy watching your own children grow, it is rewarding beyond words to watch God's newly reborn children walk through the early stages of spiritual growth. And like physical children, spiritual children grow best when lovingly nurtured by those who have come before them.

Yet a heartbreaking number of young believers are going it alone these days. They've grown up with an isolating barrage of technology that meets every need they have except the most crucial: *Being known and loved by a real live person.* And they're paying a terrible price for that gap in the form of depression, anxiety, addictions, eating disorders, cutting, and a myriad of maladies rooted in isolation.

Still, I've been pleasantly surprised at how open millennials are to genuine connection when it's sincerely offered. In the beginning, I expected my attempts at conversation to be met with awkward silence. Yet for the most part, I've found the opposite to be true.

Most millennials are willing to share quite openly, once you make the effort to treat them with respect, ask open-ended questions, and listen with genuine interest. For some reason, the social skills they struggle with in a group often spring to life quite naturally when someone makes a simple offer of friendship.

**All it takes is a little intentional effort
to leave our comfort zone and reach out without judgment.**

As Jesus said, *the harvest is plentiful but the workers are few.* Yet once you start harvesting, the experience is contagious. This crazy abundance can't quite seem to contain itself!

It doesn't just blossom in the lives of those you invest in—*it also fills you up to overflowing.* Before you know it, you're more madly in love with Jesus than ever before, and bearing fruit all over the place.

Because growth begets growth—and abundance begets abundance. As Priscilla has often reminded me: *Each time you invest the gospel in someone, its roots go deeper in you.*

This wonderful cycle of abundance becomes a way of life, until eventually the prospect of investing in "just one more" seems the most natural thing in the world to do.

Kinda like planting daisies, one handful of seeds at a time.

Because now we're learning to operate in God's generous kingdom abundance, rather than earth's stingy counterpart.

And in God's economy, there's always room for one more!

SIP 6

JESUS SAID IT, LET'S DO IT!

Christianity without discipleship
is always Christianity without Christ.
DIETRICH BONHOEFFER

Go and make disciples.
JESUS

So that's my story.

The not-so-accidental tale of an everyday believer who Jesus brought face to face with *The Great Commission*—and the fact that, for me, it had become *The Great Omission.*

Yet when I took a small step of faith forward, His truth and love came rushing in to meet me. They've been rushing in to meet me ever since, and they'll do the same for you.

All you've gotta do is start with obedience.

Not perfection.

Not "feeling" ready.

Not even wondering what's in it for you—as if making disciples was a late-night infomercial product and God had to toss in a few "extras" to sweeten the deal.

Because even though there *are* some amazing benefits to making disciples (so many, in fact, that I can't seem to get enough) the "want to" bug may not bite you right away. So sometimes it boils down to plain, old-fashioned obedience. You're a disciple of Jesus. Disciples *follow, listen, learn*—and most of all *obey.*

Jesus said,
"Go and make disciples."
MATTHEW 28:19

It's that simple. And that challenging. True transformation begins when we **do** what Jesus says—not when we hear it, agree with it, or even post it on Facebook. Yet once we take small-but-scary steps toward investing the gospel in others, *both disciple and discipler start growing like crazy.*

Over the past dozen years, my experience of the Great Commission has morphed from a dusty page in my Bible to the main reason I get up in the morning.

Knowing Christ—
and making Him known!

What could possibly compare with that?

Nothing else in all creation.

No matter how shiny or full of potential another pursuit may seem, it doesn't even come close.

All it takes is a **shift** in thinking—and a **step** of obedience.

Once that happens, there's no turning back. Because now you know that Jesus' final command describes the kind of life He intends for *every* Christian.

The life He intends for you—His beloved, blood-bought daughter who's part of His providential plan to change lives and advance His kingdom—one sip, one latte, and one loving step of obedience at a time.

Go and make disciples.

Jesus said it, let's do it!

SECOND COFFEE CHAT

Empowering
Your Story

What's Holding You Back?

If you find a path with no obstacles,
it probably doesn't lead anywhere.
FRANK A. CLARK

One act of obedience
is better than one hundred sermons.
DIETRICH BONHOEFFER

If you're still reading, chances are you're thinking—

Wow, this is amazing, how soon can I get started?

or

I want to obey, but something's still holding me back...

If you find yourself in the first group, I have surprising news. I actually *want* you to skip this *Coffee Chat*. Yep, you heard me right.

If everything inside you is crying YES, then go straight to the *Third Coffee Chat: Encouraging Her Story*. (see you there...)

But if something's still holding you back, this section is especially for you. In the next few chapters we'll look at five common roadblocks to making (or wanting to make) disciples. Each chapter is structured to help you identify and address what's holding you back from becoming the fully intentional follower of Jesus you'd *like* to be.

Before we dive in, let's invite Him into the process.

Lord Jesus, You're the last person I'd want to hold anything back from, yet there IS a part of me that still shrinks from the thought of "making disciples." You know all the reasons even better than I do. I lay them before You now—my doubts, fears, insecurities, idiosyncrasies, pride, will, and even my precious comfort zone. If You want me to make disciples, which it seems pretty clear You do, I'm asking You to give me the heart, mind, and ability to do it. Amen.

SIP 7

"I don't have time."

Making room for making disciples

*Not managing your time
and making excuses are two bad habits.
Don't put them both together
by claiming you "don't have the time."*
BO BENNETT

Okay, true confession.

I'm one of the worst time managers I know.

Don't get me wrong, it's not for lack of trying. I work at it every day with to-do lists, timers, calendars, apps, and practicing every timeliness tip I can get my hands on. Now and then I even have a day when I show up early, hit all my deadlines, and feel effortlessly drawn forward by the tranquility of the day.

(but on the other 360 days of the year, believe you me, I struggle!)

As far back as I can remember I've tended to focus so deeply on what I'm doing that I lose track of time. Guess it comes from being highly detailed *and* a born meanderer. Go ahead, do the math—it's not pretty.

Yet regardless of your time-management skills (or lack thereof), just being a living, breathing human in this computer-connected, tech-driven age can be extremely over-stimulating. Not to mention the constant pull of friends, family, work, church, hobbies, home repairs, and the never-ending need to eat, sleep, exercise, moisturize, hydrate, exfoliate, and as I mentioned before—*breathe!*

It's beyond exhausting.

So as you turn your attention to making disciples, it's only natural to feel a rising sense of panic at the very *thought* of adding one more thing to your already stuffed-to-overflowing schedule. It doesn't seem possible— or at times even healthy! Meanwhile, the solution to the "I'm too busy" issue could be staring you in the face.

Maybe your schedule needs a little pruning?

Don't worry, I'm not here to condemn. But I *am* here to shine a firm-yet-loving light in the direction of your calendar.

Would you be willing to pray this question: *Lord Jesus, are You calling me to make room for making disciples in this next season?*

If the answer is yes, trimming your schedule may not be nearly as difficult as you imagine. Here are some thought-provoking questions to get you started.

1. **Is there anything on your schedule that could easily be eliminated?** Before you roll your eyes and groan, please move on to the next suggestion. (and for the 20-30 percent of you who *did* think of something, wasn't that way easier than you expected?)

2. **Is there anything God is nudging you to do *less often* to make time for making disciples?** Sometimes you don't have to quit something entirely to clear room in your schedule. Simply switching a weekly commitment to bi-weekly or monthly can free up two to three evenings a month for spending time with a younger believer.

3. **Is there something on your schedule you find especially draining and only agreed to do out of obligation**? Maybe you've been wishing for an excuse to take it off your schedule. If so, here's the chance you've been waiting for!

Or maybe it's only a matter of getting creative.

1. **Do you know a younger believer whose schedule is similar to yours?** If so, maybe you could ask her to carpool or take lunch breaks together. Even connecting once or twice a month can make a big difference in someone's spiritual growth.

2. **Could you trade babysitting with a friend so each of you can meet with a younger believer every other week?** Or if your friend happens to *be* a younger believer, take your kids to the park together and talk about Jesus!

3. **Could you make a FaceTime date with a younger believer weekly, monthly, or quarterly** and then follow up with texts or emails in between?

The possibilities are endless. Ask the Holy Spirit to help you make "as you go" room for others within your current schedule.

SPECIAL SEASONS

At this point you might be thinking, *Aren't there ever exceptions?* Don't certain seasons of life make it nearly impossible to make room for making disciples?

Now and then, yes. Here are a few possible examples...

- When you're raising preschool children
- When you're caring for aging parents
- When you or your family are in an acute season of crisis
- When God calls you into a sabbatical season with Him

If you find yourself in a specific set-aside season, please allow me to lift that burden of condemnation right off your shoulders. Don't allow the enemy of your soul to shame you into feeling like a second-class Christian, because you're *not*. God knows the intimate details of your life, and He isn't asking you to do something you truly cannot do. That said, I encourage you to *ask* Him about it before assuming you're in a set-aside season.

A month after we moved to Nashville, I became inexplicably ill and ended up in bed for the better (or worse) part of the next year. Believe me, this was not the expansion of ministry I'd hoped for in Nashville. Midway through that bewildering year I found myself thinking, *I hate to say it, but ministry-wise, maybe God's done with me? After all, I can't do much from this bed, and there's no sign of my health getting any better.*

I wasn't officially investing in anyone at the time—in fact, I rarely left the house to even *meet* anyone to invest in.

Yet about halfway through that year, a friend of a friend suggested we start a small group Bible study for women. Before I knew it, half a dozen ladies were showing up at my house once a week for a study I was teaching! Though I was still very sick, I had just enough energy to prepare the lesson, meet with the group, and collapse back into bed.

In hindsight, I see that making time to meet with that group of women was exactly what I needed to keep growing in that near-hopeless year. Yet had I merely assumed it was a "no investment" season, I would've missed out on the huge blessing God had in store for all of us.

A few years earlier, after a devastating experience that left me heartbroken, God allowed me to disciple a young woman who was struggling with deep depression and panic attacks. At first I considered telling her I just wasn't up to it. But after asking God for wisdom, I sensed it was okay to continue—though at times I felt so emotionally crushed that, on my own, I might easily have curled up in a corner and given up.

Yet because I knew she'd be coming to my house each week, expecting me to represent Jesus, I was somehow able to hit my knees in prayer for her. I honestly believe that investing in this young woman is what kept the Holy Spirit flowing through my own wounded soul when I needed it most.

I'm happy to report that not a single week went by when God didn't show up in those meetings—though I had nothing to give her, week in and week, out for a solid year. While the primary focus of our meetings was *her* issues and not mine, looking back I can see He used that mentoring season to heal *both* of us.

Yet there have also been times when God has led me to take a break from taking on more disciples.

Bottom line, ladies, if we stay true to the season Jesus has us in (including the set-aside ones), we'll end up *where* we're supposed to be *when* we're supposed to be there. That in itself is an act of obedience.

And when the season is right, He'll be faithful to provide plenty of time for what He's called us to do: *make disciples.*

SIP 8

"I don't feel equipped."
Knowing Christ IS your competency!

*Not that we are sufficient in ourselves
to claim anything as coming from us,*

*but our sufficiency is from God,
who has made us sufficient*

*to be ministers of a new covenant,
not of the letter but of the Spirit.*

2 CORINTHIANS 3:5-6 (ESV)

Let's be honest.

Some days we feel incompetent to be a *disciple*—much less a *disciple maker*. And there's good reason for it.

*Because on our own, we **are** incompetent!*

None of us has what it takes to follow Christ perfectly or model that out for someone else. Even the greatest pastor, counselor, or teacher has moments of failure and self-doubt. That's part of being human. I've even heard women from the above disciplines question whether *they* are qualified to be disciplers.

But thanks be to God, the defining quality for making disciples *isn't* limitless knowledge or flawless perfection. *The defining quality of an effective discipler is a life-giving connection to the risen Christ, and a willingness to help others experience the same.*

The rest can be learned.

So no matter how incompetent you may feel—*or in some areas, even be*—the bigger truth is...

Your relationship with Christ IS your competency!

And God's Word is your guide to help you live out that "Christ-competency" day by day.

53

YOUR STORY

Your testimony is the story of what Christ has done for you. It's also part of your *credential* for making disciples. Your story gives others a sense of your history with Jesus, and reminds you of where your power and competency come from. You may not think your story is all that spectacular. For years, I didn't. Having met Jesus when I was in elementary school, I didn't have much of a pre-salvation tale to tell.

Boy oh boy, I really went on a juice-box bender last night—I must've drunk a whole six-pack! (not that they even come in six-packs *or* that I even drank them as a child—but I digress)

Two or three decades of living later, my "here's what Jesus did for me" story became much more dramatic. Yet either way, I *still* had a story worth telling. *And so do you.* If Jesus is the center of your life, then your story is full of awe and wonder:

- *The King of all kings knows and loves you intimately.*
- *He bought you back with the price of His blood.*
- *He gave you a clean slate and a brand new identity.*
- *He's preparing you to rule and reign with Him forever.*
- *Now that, my friend, is a STORY!*

For that matter, there's also no reason to feel unworthy because your B.C. story feels "too bad" to be a good testimony. Not a single thing on the path God has led you down—the good, bad, or even the "boring"—is ever wasted.

If you struggle to believe that, check out Romans 8:28 or Isaiah 61:3. Plus, Revelation 12 says: "They overcame him by the blood of the lamb and the word of their testimony."

Whether your God-story reads like a childhood conversion or a Lifetime Movie of the Week, it's *still* a powerful story. And there's someone out there who desperately needs to hear it.

GOD'S WORD

The Bible is our primary source of truth for making disciples. But since many believers feel insecure about their biblical knowledge, they don't even try. Yet helping someone get established in their faith means returning to the basics, which you probably have more knowledge of than you realize.

For example, you may know a fair amount of Scriptural truth, but just can't quote the chapter and verse. These days, that's not a big deal. Just do an internet search for the part of the verse you *can* remember, or type in "verses about such and such" and let Google do the searching for you. Then plug the reference it gives you into whatever Bible app you prefer—and now you can read the verse for yourself!

There are also plenty of online Bible study tools available, not to mention fill-in-the-blank Bible studies galore you could walk through with someone—even if you're not an expert on the particular passage yourself.

God will be faithful to equip you, as you are willing to take small steps of faith forward.

COMPETENT IN CHRIST

The bottom line is that many of us have believed a lie.

We've believed that making disciples is for perfect Christians with spectacular testimonies, and we simply do not qualify. So we often self-terminate before we even begin.

Yet you don't have to live with that "I could never do this" status one minute longer. *The truth is, the privilege of spiritual reproduction is meant for every believer*—and that, my friend, means you!

- *God has declared you eligible.*
- *Your connection with Jesus qualifies you.*
- *Anything you don't know can be learned.*
- *You can invest the gospel in others, starting today.*

Just share **what** you know with **who** you know—*and trust God to teach you more as you go!*

SIP 9

"What if I get in over my head?"

You'll be stretched, and God will provide!

But he said to me,
"My grace is sufficient for you,
for my power is made perfect in weakness."
2 CORINTHIANS 12:9

If you never get in over your head,
how will you ever learn to swim?
ANONYMOUS

One of the scariest things about making disciples is: *What if something happens I'm not prepared for? And what if that "something" is something I know nothing about?*

This seems to be everyone's worst fear.

And I've definitely been there.

The first girl I met with was bipolar, only she didn't realize it, yet so she was self-medicating with recreational drugs. The next girl collapsed into my arms at our first official meeting and sobbed, "Oh Kim, last night I slept with a total stranger!"

"In over your head" moments, to say the least.

Since I had no experience with making disciples, or the particular issues these girls struggled with, all I could do was send up a quick prayer and love the person in front of me.

Which didn't turn out to be nearly as scary as I expected.

Because God was faithful.

When I needed answers He provided them, though admittedly I often wasn't quite sure what to say until I heard the words come out of my mouth. Other times I sensed His grace and guidance to simply be there in the process with them, without saying much at all.

Yet moment by moment, and inch by inch, the Holy Spirit doled out generous helpings of godly common sense.

- *Listen with all your heart...*
- *Teach her about boundaries...*
- *Make a joke to lighten the mood...*
- *Encourage her to seek medical help...*
- *Hug her and let her cry it out, that's what she needs...*

I'm not saying I did everything perfectly. Sometimes I missed a cue or zigged when I should've zagged. But Jesus never did. He always gave me enough clarity and strength to love the person in front of me and stay the course.

Fortunately, not all spiritual mentoring scenarios are nearly as dramatic as the two examples above. Most of the time they follow a much more predictable path, with day-by-day growth and steady progress forward. Yet now and then you too will find yourself in a situation you didn't quite see coming.

And it's okay—that's part of the adventure!

That's where our faithful "I will be with you" Jesus comes into the process.

And He *never* misses a cue.

OVERWHELM PREVENTION

A while back I was talking with my husband about this chapter and he suddenly asked, "Well, isn't that the goal? To get them in over their head as soon as possible?" I threw back my head and laughed, because it dawned on me that IS the goal!

Getting in over your head is a great way to learn. And no matter how much you fear sinking in the sea of uncertainty, Jesus will always be there to give you a hand and keep you afloat.

Yet experience has also taught me that *some kinds of "in over your head" experiences aren't necessary,* and can even be counter-productive. Thankfully, they can be lessened or eliminated with a little godly wisdom.

Here are some examples...

1. **Wait until she's mentor-ready.**

   While there will always be unknowns in the spiritual mentoring process, there are also some easily recognizable traits present in those whose hearts and lives are what I call **mentor-ready**. It's best not to rush into meeting with someone regularly until you see those traits in her and God gives you the green light.

Until then, continue to love, encourage, and pray for her on a more informal basis whenever you happen to cross paths. I've often seen this approach lead to mentor-readiness down the line, while sparing both of you the stress of trying to "make" something happen before she's truly ready. *(see "Sip 14: Deciding Who to Disciple" for more details)*

2. Know yourself / Know your boundaries.

I've found it's helpful to set a few spiritual mentoring boundaries *before* the fact.

For example, if teaching isn't your gift, making a decision to use fill-in-the-blank Bible studies can prevent overwhelm and increase your confidence.

Or if you already know you have limited time to meet, letting your mentee know that up front prevents unmet expectations for her and over-commitment for you.

Being proactive about a few basic boundaries from the beginning is a great way to avoid overwhelm.

3. Partner with others.

Just as a primary care physician refers patients to a specialist, a wise spiritual mentor knows she doesn't need to do everything herself.

For example, if you're not comfortable counseling someone through a deep emotional crisis, don't worry. There are those in the body of Christ who are trained for that very thing—and love doing it.

Or maybe the woman you're meeting with has an interest in an area of ministry you know nothing about, such as working with inner city youth or rescuing young women from human trafficking. Connecting her with someone else with experience in that area could be just the thing she needs to get started. Again, you don't have to do it all. *(see "Sip 13: Setting Loving Limits" for more details)*

SWIMMING LESSONS

Ever get thrown in the pool before you could swim?

Terrifying, right?

Yet the next time you get in over your head, something new happens: *You remember you didn't drown the first time!*

The same is true with the spiritual mentoring process. In a strange-yet-awful way, that "oh no, I'm gonna drown" feeling goes a long way toward (you guessed it) learning to swim.

Why?

Because we have to venture *past* our known limits if we ever want to *exceed* them.

You'll be stretched—and God will provide.

Don't let fear hold you back from the adventure of a lifetime. Jesus has called you. You can do this. And the Holy Spirit is oh-so-willing to help.

So jump on in, the water's fine!

SIP 10

"I'm still waiting to be mentored."

God has not forgotten you!

*See, I have engraved you
on the palms of my hands;
your walls are ever before me.*
ISAIAH 49:16

Dear daughter of the King, your Father could *never* forget you.

Jesus' nail-scarred hands are proof of that.

Yet I know what it's like to feel overlooked, forgotten, or hidden in plain sight. For four-plus decades of my life, I longed to feel truly *seen* by someone who'd take the time to invest in me. So I realize what a difficult thing I'm asking. I'm asking you to give to others the very thing you wish you'd received.

Yet ultimately, it isn't me who's asking.

It's Jesus.

The One who promised you He'd never leave you or forsake you, and then etched your name on the palms of His hands to prove it.

Precious one, I promise you this...

**Jesus loves you every bit as much
as the ones He's asking you to invest in.**

He sees how faithfully you've followed Him and knows how forgotten you sometimes feel. Yet He still has a plan and you're *still* part of it! Without the love and nurture of those who have gone before them, a whole generation is at risk of watering down the gospel or walking away from faith in Christ completely.

When the next great harvest of new believers comes (and I believe it will), who will disciple them if we don't? You and I have a choice to make. We can step up and answer God's call, or watch it skip an entire generation—*the one we're responsible for.*

While being asked to give what you didn't receive feels unjust, the reality is: *someone has to go first.* And we are privileged to be part of that bridge generation.

> *The harvest is plentiful but the workers are few.*
> *Ask the Lord of the harvest, therefore,*
> *to send out workers into His harvest field.*
> LUKE 10:2; MATTHEW 9:37-38

Yet Jesus is also asking for a far more *personal* reason.

He's asking because He doesn't want you to miss out on the abundance!

I'm living proof of the full-circle joy that comes from accepting Jesus' challenge to make disciples, even when you *think* your own time for being discipled has come and gone. He's more than able to fill your mentor gap—and your cup to overflowing—even in the midst of being asked to give what you haven't yet received. (emphasis on *yet...*)

So the question is not, "Have I been discipled?" Because for the overwhelming majority, the answer is no.

The question to ask is...

Am I truly His disciple?
A devoted follower, a learner at His feet?

If the answer is YES, then it's time to step out in faith.

He hasn't forgotten you. You won't be left behind. And I believe you *will* be rewarded for going first. His beautiful nail-scarred hands are reaching out to you even now.

As you trust Him to fill your mentor gap in *His* way and *His* time...

Jesus Himself
will be the mentor you've always longed for!

SIP 11

"To be honest - I just can't want to."

It's a gift wrapped in a command.

If you want to change,
you must be willing to be uncomfortable.
UNKNOWN

My friend's toddler was an obedient little fellow. But one day when she asked him to do something especially difficult, he shook his head and wailed, "No-no-no! I can't want to!" But then, marshaling every bit of willpower he possessed, he proceeded to do exactly what she asked.

Pretty profound stuff for a two-year-old.

Because as every grown-up two-year-old knows, that's often the heart of the problem.

We just can't want to!

Try as we might, many of us struggle with the embarrassing fact that our deep-down "want to" doesn't always line up with the things God says we "ought to." Things like Bible reading, praying, fasting, serving, giving, evangelizing, and yep, you guessed it—discipling.

If we're gut-level honest, *sometimes we're just not feelin' it.*

So we skulk around like a kid without her homework, hoping against hope the teacher won't call on us.

Yet lately I've come to realize that every "thou shalt" in the Bible is a gift wrapped in a command.

Come again?

Let me rephrase that.

Each of God's commands contains a hidden gift—
and obedience is how we unwrap it!

Here are a few examples...

COMMAND:	*Be grateful.*
GIFT:	Encouragement / renewed focus / resilience

COMMAND:	*Don't lie.*
GIFT:	Peace of mind / self-respect / being trusted by others

COMMAND:	*Don't work on the Sabbath.*
GIFT:	Renewal / rest / weekly "reset" button

COMMAND:	*Go and make disciples.*
GIFT:	Accelerated growth / connection / purpose / legacy

TASTE AND SEE

Psalm 34:8 invites us to "taste and see that the Lord is good."

When we bump up against a big wall of *can't want to,* the only path to the other side is trusting our Abba enough to take a risk. Like a child who hates veggies, we must be willing to try the broccoli. We must taste and see.

Of course, we can always refuse to obey. We can hold back. Yet if we do, we take an even bigger risk. We risk missing out on the reward of an overflowing life, the adventure of bringing God's kingdom to earth, and the wholehearted "well done" of our Heavenly Father when we see Him face to face.

Yet all it takes to obey is inching your way forward one simple-yet-intentional cup of coffee at a time. I hope you'll decide to a take a risk and choose the "taste and see" option.

'Cuz I'm telling you right now—*it's pretty yummy delicious!*

SIP 12

Loved to Overflowing

You were MADE for this!

Obedience to God is the pathway
to the life you really want to live.
JOYCE MEYER

Making disciples is the art of letting God's love fill you up so completely that it spills over into others' lives quite (super) naturally.

When you love Him back, that love increases.

When you share it with others, it multiplies.

Yet it's difficult to give away God's love if you have trouble receiving it in the first place.

LOVE BLOCKAGES

Sometimes the way we think about God and ourselves creates a blockage between us, just as cholesterol clogs an artery.

Maybe you think some things in your past are too awful to forgive. Or it's difficult to imagine God ever loving you quite the same, even if He did forgive you.

Maybe you've kept God at a polite distance for years, for reasons even you don't fully understand. Of course you respect Him and obey Him, and you know He's officially "good" and "righteous." But the prospect of a close emotional connection with Him feels foreign or scary—maybe even impossible.

If what I just described feels strangely familiar, let me ask you something.

Do you have young children in your life? (kids, grandkids, nieces, nephews) If so, why do you love them? What is it about their messy, whiney, peanut-butter-covered, "me-me-mine" little selves that leaves you feeling so enamored?

Ah, I see. They're sweet, adorable, and give you hugs and kisses whenever the mood strikes them. Yeah, that's pretty compelling.

But let me ask you this.

In a different mood, wouldn't they just as soon pummel you with oatmeal as look at you? Don't they also try your patience, spend your money, hurt your feelings, and drive you to the point of distraction?

Yet when push comes to shove, the bottom-line reason most parents give for why they love their children is simple: *Because they're mine.*

Right?

So let me ask you this: *Why should your Heavenly Father feel any different about you?*

You're made in His image. You're a priceless original. You're His beloved one-of-a-kind daughter, created to be the object of His boundless affection. He knows you by name, delights in you, and longs to have intimate friendship with you—warts, bruises, sins, mistakes, peanut-buttery fingers and all.

And because He loves you, He *also* loves that pouring into others will increase your joy and accelerate your growth like nothing else—because a flowing river is always more full of life than a stagnant pond.

**And nothing but loved-to-overflowing abundance
will do for His precious blood-bought girls!**

IT'S YOUR TURN

This little book's rather lofty goal is to launch you into the very kind of life you were *made* for.

Helping others walk out their redemption was meant to be part of your full-circle experience in Christ. The Father knew that helping others "press enter" on their relationship with Jesus would deepen your own roots in Him and provide exactly the kind of far-reaching legacy your heart longs for.

So what are you waiting for?

Like a mighty army of pedicured warriors, let's drink in His truth, feed on His love, and follow our General into the spiritual battle we were born for.

Let's go and make disciples!

THIRD COFFEE CHAT

*Encouraging
Her Story*

COFFEE DATE SKILLS

Back Pocket Basics

For we are His workmanship,
created in Christ Jesus for good works,
which God prepared beforehand that we should walk in them.
EPHESIANS 2:10 (NKJV)

Good conversation is just as stimulating as coffee,
and just as hard to sleep after.
ANNE MORROW LINDBERGH

If Jesus walked the earth today, I'm guessing He'd spend a fair amount of time at Starbucks. Can't you picture Him relaxing at a cozy table, latte in hand, talking with thirsty souls about what truly satisfies?

(drinking decaf of course—or maybe He has a higher caffeine tolerance?)

Many a business mentor has met with a protégé at Starbucks.

What if you were there to be mentored by Jesus?

Talk about mind-blowing insights and spot-on instruction! Yet that's exactly the offer Jesus is making to each of His disciples. And, in part, He's making His offer through you and me.

Before you panic, let me assure you, you've been *fully* equipped and He'll *never* leave your side for a minute.

When two or three of you are together because of me,
you can be sure that I'll be there.
MATTHEW 18:20 (MSG)

At the heart of it, making disciples is as simple as a conversation. You, her, and Jesus—having coffee. And almost everyone can find time for a cup of coffee. *So if you know Jesus, and you can do coffee, you can do discipleship!*

Back pocket basics are *learnable relational skills* that enable any believer to turn a *good conversation* into a *God-conversation*. And once meaningful God-conversations become a habit, just add authentic obedience and friendly follow-up—and you've got discipleship!

GIVE 'EM JESUS

He's the answer to every question...

John 14:6 | Colossians 1:27

Early in my spiritual mentoring journey, I stumbled onto a liberating truth.

I wasn't the actual discipler!

Jesus Himself was very much in attendance, bringing details to light, turning the conversation this way or that, and gently but firmly calling the shots as only a Master Discipler could.

There weren't two of us talking.

There were *three*.

It was also clear that Jesus and His disciple had a shared history together, whether long or short, which I was now being invited to share. It made perfect sense that He would be speaking to His own disciple! *How had I missed that before?*

This realization forever changed how I "made" disciples. Since then, my primary focus has been helping each woman observe and obey what Jesus is *already* highlighting in her life, rather than me dictating what she ought to learn at any given moment.

This "ask Jesus" approach teaches her the habit of listening for His voice first, even (and especially) before asking her discipler. This is great news for first-time disciplers, because it means you don't have to know all the answers!

Jesus is the Coach—you're the spotter.

Your job is simply to stay *connected* with the Master Discipler and keep *pointing* her back to Him.

Be a faithful coffee-cup ambassador, and He'll do the rest.

When in doubt, give 'em Jesus!

HENRY DRUMMOND: *Every character has an inward spring; let Christ be that spring. Every action has a keynote; let Christ be that note, to which your whole life is attuned.*

C.S. LEWIS: *I know now, Lord, why you utter no answer. You are yourself the answer.*

AUTHENTICITY
Just be you, filled with Jesus...

John 1:47 | Ecclesiastes 3:7*b*

Authenticity is a fancy way of saying—be yourself.

Being yourself enables you to connect with the specific people God has uniquely equipped you to serve.

**Authenticity is one of the
secret ingredients of discipleship.**

It's a crucial enzyme that makes it possible for us to digest truth in a real, down-to-earth way.

That's exactly how God designed it to work.

He uses our good, bad, and "messy-middle" moments to produce empathy, camaraderie, and ever-increasing growth in the body of Christ.

That said, I do have one gentle word of caution. There's a huge difference between being authentic in a healthy way, and emotionally dumping on someone. As disciplers, our highest priority is to be ambassadors of Christ's love and protect the spiritual growth of the younger believers entrusted to our care.

So here's a helpful question to ask yourself.

**Will sharing this specific detail
help or hinder her spiritual growth?**

Now and then, despite your best efforts to share only what's helpful, an attempt at authenticity may get away from you and morph into an accidental over-share.

If this happens, don't panic. Simply own your error, and ask for her forgiveness. While this may be awkward at first, God's grace is well able to cover your mistake and turn it into a teachable moment.

Plus, over the years I've noticed a couple of encouraging patterns.

1. About 90 percent of the times I've felt the need to check in with someone about a potential over-share, it turns out she either a) didn't notice it, or b) experienced it as a good thing!

Common reply:
"It was actually a *relief* to know you struggle too."

2. God seems to use these awkward check-in conversations as a kind of *spiritual fertilizer.* It turns out the person I over-shared with almost always experiences a noticeable growth spurt soon afterwards!

Common result:
"You know, after we talked I got to thinking..."

So whether you do it perfectly or not, authenticity still spurs growth!
What a comfort to know that even our occasional "oops" can be turned for good in the skillful hands of the Master Discipler.

Authenticity Rules of Thumb

It can be helpful to keep these questions in mind as you model authenticity for the person you're mentoring.

Transparency

1. Am I being honest about my own strengths and weaknesses, or am I trying to make myself sound more spiritual than I actually am?

2. Am I interacting with her in a way that models authenticity and encourages mutual love and support?

Discretion

1. Is she mature enough to hear this right now? Or is it likely to be confusing, overwhelming, or distracting?

2. What is the Holy Spirit saying to me about this conversation? Is He nudging me to be transparent or cautioning me to exercise discretion?

MOTHER TERESA: *Honesty and transparency make you vulnerable. Be honest and transparent anyway.*

BRENE BROWN: *That's everything I know about vulnerability. It's not winning, it's not losing, it's showing up and being seen.*

LISTENING

The rare gift of paying attention...

James 1:19

If we're honest, most of us would rather talk than listen.

I must confess, this is especially true of me.

I'm a born talker!

My mom tells me I was an extremely verbal baby who memorized nursery rhymes and spoke in full sentences by the time I was a year old. She spent long hours cultivating my "talk-ability" which I enjoyed so much I've rarely taken a breath since.

Over the years, I've talked more people under the table than I care to admit. I'd rather talk than eat, sleep, rest, or play. In fact, one of my favorite quotes is: "How can I know what I think till I see what I say?" (E.M. Forster)

Yet in recent years I've learned something very valuable.

I was also born to listen.

And so were you.

Listening is essential to spiritual mentoring
because it gives you a *window* into a person's heart.

As the New Testament puts it, "Lead with your ears, follow up with your tongue" (James 1:19 [MSG]).

Do I hear a collective sigh of relief from the introverts?

You mean I don't have to do all the talking? Perfect!

By showing up and listening, you're *already* investing Christ's love in a powerful way. There's a better-than-average chance the person in front of you has never experienced this kind of focused listening before.

You can give her the gift of Christ's love
poured through you—simply by paying attention.

Being listened to from the heart has a wonderfully transforming effect. The rigid become relaxed, the timid become talkative, and the upset become uplifted. It may not happen all at once, but if you keep at it you'll be amazed at the transforming power of truly listening.

Becoming a better listener takes practice and plenty of trial and error. A dozen years into the process, I'm still learning ways to improve my *loving listening* skills.

Yet even when we listen imperfectly, God graciously blesses the process. Taking time to hear another's heart is the best way I know to communicate love *and* grow to love someone more deeply. It's a two-for-the-price-of-one kind of blessing!

Now and then as I'm listening to one of God's girls, her countenance seems to take on a sort of holy glow. It's difficult to explain yet impossible to forget once you've experienced it. It's as if for one brief moment I'm allowed to glimpse the God-given glory of who she's becoming. Each time it happens, I'm left speechless with wonder.

Nothing else compares to watching a child of God come fully alive from the inside out.

And to think it starts with something as simple as listening.

Listening not only with your mind, or even your emotions, but letting the Holy Spirit listen *through* you. As a wise counselor once observed, it's getting to be "a holy witness" (Vincent Staraci).

What a rarity it is to meet a fellow traveler who's willing to give the gift of paying attention.

ERNEST HEMINGWAY: *When people talk, listen completely. Most people never listen.*

ARGENTINE PROVERB: *Who speaks, sows; who listens, reaps.*

LEARN-ABILITY

If you don't know, learn it together!

Proverbs 9:9

One of the biggest hurdles to making disciples is, *What if she asks me something and I don't know the answer?* This terrifying question has drained courage from the heart of many a would-be mentor.

Yet in most cases, new disciples ask questions involving foundational truths and skills you've long since mastered, or ones that can be easily learned by both of you together.

It's perfectly okay to learn new things
right alongside your mentee!

All it takes is a dash of humility—and a little effort.

After all, what can't be googled, right? You can find Bible translations, articles, study tools, videos, and pretty much anything you can imagine at the click of a mouse. It's all there for the asking.

Plus, the Holy Spirit will be there to guide you as you seek the truth together. It's like a heavenly scavenger hunt, with the Holy Spirit guiding you, Jesus dropping clues, and the Father waiting at the last house saying, *See, I knew you could do it!*

None of us will ever cease to be an apprentice of Christ, so learning alongside those we mentor is great practice for a lifetime of learning. It also nips in the bud those ugly fears of not "getting it right" and models humility and learn-ability in a very practical way.

That is, if we're willing to swallow our pride and say the seven most freeing words in Christendom: "I don't know...let's learn it together!"

EARTHA KITT: *I am learning all the time. The tombstone will be my diploma.*

JOHN WOODEN: *It's what you learn after you know it all that counts.*

MODELING

More is caught than taught...

I Peter 5:3

Ever been to an exercise class with those giant floor-to-ceiling mirrors? Their stated purpose is to help you improve your form by matching it with the instructor's.

(does out-of-breath-super-slow-mo count as form?)

Minus the spandex, that's how spiritual mentoring works. A new disciple learns by doing and observing—at the same time.

As she learns to walk with Jesus, she's also watching how you approach your work, love your family, depend on God, respond to His Word, interact with others, and handle a rough day. I think she's especially paying attention to that. She needs to see that even though you're not perfect, you're being molded and shaped by the same Lord who's at work in her life.

**Living out godly principles is a silent "amen"
to every truth a mentor teaches.**

She desperately needs to see your example, because the world around her is modeling something vastly different. By and large, the boundaries and values of her friends are *not* based on the same Kingdom principles she's learning from you. So she's watching and wondering if living by the Bible is even possible.

(she may not let on she's watching—but trust me, she is)

And when she catches a glimpse of Him in your life (even in your oh-so-human frailties), she'll have the evidence she needs to build her life on Christ.

ALBERT SCHWEITZER: *Example is not the main thing in influencing others. It is the only thing.*

RALPH WALDO EMERSON: *What you do speaks so loudly that I cannot hear what you say.*

ACCOUNTABILITY

Permission to hold up a loving mirror...

James 1:23-25 | Proverbs 27:17

The book of James says if we *hear* the Word but don't *do* it, we're like a person who walks away from a mirror and forgets what she looks like.

Yet sometimes we need help seeing our reflection clearly. A mentor is in a unique position to hold up a loving mirror without shaming us in the process, especially in those blind spot areas that are tough to recognize on our own.

Once she does, we may not always like what we see. Yet having a "mirror mentor" in our life, who loves us no matter what, can help *cushion* the blow and give us *courage* to surrender those blind spot areas to Jesus.

Yet a mirror should never be shoved in anyone's face.

**As spiritual mentors, we only have as much
authority in someone's life as they *give* us.**

One of the best ways to put a *strain* on your mentoring relationship is insisting on a level of accountability you haven't both agreed to. Holding someone accountable works much better as an *invitation* rather than a demand. Even God, who has every right to require accountability from us, doesn't force His way into our lives—but waits to be invited.

Yet when a mentor has earned the right to be heard by authentically listening, learning, and modeling—receiving and heeding a firm-yet-gentle word of correction becomes a whole lot easier.

Many people avoid accountability for fear of being bullied or judged. If you've had a bad experience with authority in the past, this is a valid concern. Yet what I'm suggesting is quite the opposite. Godly accountability is respectful, humble, and helpful—not harsh, critical, or bossy.

When voluntary accountability is firing on all cylinders, it accelerates growth—*because you get the benefit of two perspectives for the price of one!* Plus, you have a built-in partner to cheer you on...

BOB PROCTOR: *Accountability is the glue that ties commitment to results.*

STEPHEN COVEY: *Accountability breeds response-ability.*

PRAYER

God's gift that keeps on giving...

Ephesians 6:18 | Philippians 1:6

In my experience, two kinds of prayer are useful for spiritual mentoring.

Praying with Her

One of my favorite things is witnessing the beautifully unique way each daughter of the King expresses her heart in prayer. It's like overhearing an intimate moment between the Master Artist and His emerging masterpiece.

Not only are you privileged to hear what impacts her heart most deeply, you also get to share in the drama and delight of watching God answer her requests, one by one.

When you pray with a disciple, you also allow her to hear you petition the Lord on her behalf. Hearing someone pray for you can feel a bit awkward at first. Yet this kind of three-way communion between heaven and earth plants your friendship firmly in God's Presence.

**Praying with someone takes you deeper
than a conversation ever could.**

Beginning and ending your conversations with prayer gives God free reign to lead, guide, and empower your times together as He wishes.

Praying for Her

One of the beauties of prayer is that you don't have to be physically present with someone to lift them before the Father.

Whenever the Spirit brings her to mind— is a great time to pray!

If you wish, you can set aside a certain day each week or month to pray. Or you might want to adopt the habit of briefly praying for her whenever you exchange texts or emails. Allow the Holy Spirit to guide you into an intercession pattern that works best for you.

Another beauty of prayer is its availability for *every* stage of the mentoring relationship.

Whether you're still meeting (or not), you can pray.
Whether she's receptive to your input (or not), you can pray.
Whether you stay connected (or lose touch), you can pray.
Whether she's living nearby (or halfway around the world), you can pray.

Prayer is one of the most powerful weapons in your mentoring arsenal. Any time of the day or night, prayer enables you to fight for her in the spiritual realm and know with confidence that God will hear and answer. It's like having a spiritual SWAT team at your disposal!

CHARLES SPURGEON: *No man can do me a truer kindness in this world than to pray for me.*

HUDSON TAYLOR: *Pray for those you send, shield them by prayer.*

Review: BACK POCKET BASICS

God has already placed the spiritual mentoring tools you need right there in your back pocket!

- ❑ **G: GIVE 'EM JESUS** He's the Answer to Every Question
- ❑ **A: AUTHENTICITY** Just be You, Filled with Jesus
- ❑ **L: LISTENING** The Rare Gift of Paying Attention
- ❑ **L: LEARN-ABILITY** If You Don't Know, Learn it Together!
- ❑ **M: MODELING** More is Caught than Taught
- ❑ **A: ACCOUNTABILITY** Permission to Hold Up a Loving Mirror
- ❑ **P: PERSISTENT PRAYER** God's Gift that Keeps on Giving

(see Appendix for "Back Pocket Basics" worksheet)

Memorizing this simple acronym may help you to remember...

GAL MAP

a relational map for discipling women

If you feel rusty or inexperienced in any of these areas, allow yourself some time to **ponder** and **practice** them in everyday life.

Just pick the relational skill you need to practice, ask the Holy Spirit for help, and love the person in front of you. With each new experience, your confidence will grow.

(even if you make mistakes—which is part of the process)

Rest assured, Jesus has given you the **back pocket basics** you need to become an effective coffee-date discipler!

SIP 13

SETTING LOVING LIMITS

Coffee is not my cup of tea.
SAMUEL GOLDWYN

Once we accept our limits,
we go beyond them.
ALBERT EINSTEIN

In our 24/7 drive-through world, the words *loving* and *limits* may sound like direct opposites. Yet the two work best hand in hand.

Loving limits serve a dual purpose.

They protect spiritual mentors from over-commitment and burnout, and provide mentees with a safe place to learn and grow.

SPIRITUAL SCAFFOLDING

In the construction world, **physical scaffolding** provides workers with safety, stability, and ease of access while building a structure. In a similar way, **spiritual scaffolding** provides safety, stability, and ease of access to each area of a disciple's life (or foundation) that's being rebuilt on Christ.

Spiritual scaffolding makes it possible to safely and steadily connect with growth-ready areas of a person's heart through intentional conversation, listening, questions, brainstorming, Bible study, prayer, action steps, and gentle accountability.

Without a few simple structures in place, mentoring conversations tend to ramble aimlessly. With them, it's much easier for mentor and mentee to stay consistently connected and stay on track with each area of growth God is walking them through together.

YOUR BOUNDARIES

There are two kind of loving limits you're going to need: *yours and hers.* Let's start with yours. It's best to give your own loving limits some thought *before* you start meeting with someone.

Here are three categories to consider...

❏ **Time Commitment**
❏ **Mentoring Style**
❏ **Refilling the Well**

(see Appendix for "Setting Loving Limits—Mentor" worksheet)

Let's look at each of these briefly.

Time Commitment

Spiritual mentoring is not a one-size-fits-all proposition. It's important to prayerfully decide what is suitable and sustainable for this season of your life. You will do yourself a huge favor by thinking through a few things in advance.

- **Which days and times work best for me?**
- **Can I meet weekly, bi-weekly, or monthly?**
- **Ideally, how long would each meeting last?**
- **Am I comfortable with emailing and texting in between? Or phone calls?** *(it's better to say no now than regret it later)*
- **Do I have any early/late time parameters?** *("I need our meetings to end by 9" or "no calls before 7 am")*

The possibilities are endless.

(but your meetings don't have to be!)

If you take time to **prayerfully decide your boundaries in advance**, you'll be better prepared to coordinate your schedule with hers.

Mentoring Style

In the Bible, each mentoring relationship had its own unique flavor. Jesus and the disciples, Paul and Timothy, Moses and Joshua, Elijah and Elisha, Naomi and Ruth.

In each instance, the *message* was unchanging but the *method* was flexible. Always keep in mind that spiritual mentoring is a relationship, not a program, so the more personal the better.

Here are three areas to ponder regarding your own mentoring style...

- Your own gifting / comfort level
- Her mentoring needs
- How you sense the Lord leading

And remember whatever style you choose, your **back pocket basics** will serve you well.

G: Give 'em Jesus
A: Authenticity
L: Listening
L: Learn-ability
M: Modeling
A: Accountability
P: Prayer

Beyond that, the sky's the limit.

Take some time to brainstorm your **loving limits** before you get started. Think practical, get creative, and remember that your discipleship style doesn't have to look like anybody else's. God has declared you competent—you can do this.

So choose your style, make a coffee date, and take your first sip!

Refilling the Well

Another loving limit you can set for yourself is the habit of refilling your spiritual well regularly. It's easy to get so caught up doing the work of the Lord that we forget how **utterly dependent** we are on the Lord of the work.

Those of us who have committed ourselves to letting God flow through us must continually return to Him for **refilling** and **renewal**. So before you start discipling others, here are a few questions to ask yourself.

- Am I getting enough **unhurried time** with God each day?
- Do I have a plan in place for **reading the Word**?
- Do I have a couple of **Aaron and Hur friends** who could hold my arms up in prayer as I set out on this discipleship journey?

Benjamin Franklin wisely observed that an ounce of prevention is worth a pound of cure. The best way to prevent burnout is to get in the habit of refilling your own well regularly.

It's also a tangible reminder that we as disciplers are merely *conduits* of God's truth and love, NOT the source.

HER EXPECTATIONS

Now that you've made some pre-decisions about your own boundaries, you're ready to share them with the person you'll be discipling—which leads quite naturally to talking with her about her own needs and expectations for spiritual mentoring.

- ❑ **How often does she want to meet?**
- ❑ **What days and times work for her schedule?**
- ❑ **What style of mentoring is she looking for?** *(weekly coffee chats, fill-in-the-blank Bible study, shared activities, etc.)*
- ❑ **What is she hoping to see God do in her life through the spiritual mentoring process?**

Here's a scaffolding checklist to help you get started...

- ❑ **WHEN:** How often / how long will you meet?
- ❑ **WHERE:** What location works best for both of you?
- ❑ **WHY:** What is her motivation for discipleship?
- ❑ **WHAT:** What areas does she hope to grow in?
- ❑ **HOW #1:** Goals? Methods? Accountability?
- ❑ **HOW #2:** How will we know when we're finished?

(see Appendix for "Setting Loving Limits—Mentor + Mentee" worksheet)

Talking through these simple scaffolding questions during your first meeting or two will help set the tone for your mentoring relationship. It's a practical way to make her a priority and model healthy boundaries.

Loving limits benefit both parties.

They provide her with a safe place to learn and grow, and help you keep your own cup filled to overflowing.

SIP 14

DECIDING
WHO TO DISCIPLE

Whether you turn to the right or to the left,
your ears will hear a voice behind you, saying,
"This is the way; walk in it."
ISAIAH 30:21

Be brave enough
to start a conversation that matters.
DAU VOIRE

Now that you've dusted off your **back pocket basics** and set **loving limits**, you're ready to find someone to disciple!

As a first-time discipler, you'll probably relate to one of these three "finding" scenarios.

1. **I have NO idea where to begin.**

    If this is how you feel, you're not alone. That's how everyone feels at first. Take a deep breath and keep reading for some step-by-step principles for discovering and recognizing the person God wants you to mentor.

2. **My church has a mentoring ministry.**

    If your church already has a mentoring ministry in place, you're in great shape. Just sign up and follow whatever steps they give you, which will usually include some sort of mentor training. (feel free to keep reading for basic principles though!)

3. **I have someone in mind, but I'm not sure.**

    In this chapter, we'll talk about some practical ways to find out if the person you have in mind is "mentor-ready." This will help prevent a multitude of mishaps and give you the best chance possible for a healthy mentoring relationship.

Regardless of your "finding" scenario, all first-time mentors have one thing in common: *We hope to find someone we click with.*

And why not? Discipleship is a very personal and relational process, so the experience is much richer if both parties feel a kindredness of spirit. That's why I love letting God Himself be the one to connect us.

GOD ALREADY KNOWS HER NAME

You may not have the foggiest idea who or where she is, but God is looking into her sweet face at this very moment, and knows exactly what kind of mentor she needs. He's also looking into your heart, and is well aware of the kind of mentor He designed you to be.

And He's quite adept at bringing the two together!

I've seen Him do it time and again, as I simply show up and follow His lead.

5 Steps to Finding

Finding someone to disciple is about being *led* by the Spirit, rather than anxiously searching for her on your own. Here are five common-sense principles God has taught me through trial and error that I hope will bring you peace during those "how will I ever recognize her" moments.

Following these guidelines makes it much easier to sit back, enjoy the ride, and allow God to do the "finding."

STEP 1: Ask God for guidance.

This one seems obvious, right?

Yet you'd be surprised how easy it is to skip this step.

We get all excited, rush out the door, and before we know it we're straining and striving in our own strength to find the "right" person. It's much less stressful to let God do the finding for you.

Consider praying something like this...

Lord, You already know the name of the young woman you want me to disciple. You've known her from the foundation of the world, just as You've known me. I'm trusting You to connect us at just the right time, and to help us recognize each other. Thank you Lord...I can't wait to meet her!

STEP 2: Who's in your *oikos*?

Unless you walk around speaking Greek, **oikos** probably isn't a word you're familiar with. Me neither, until I heard Tom Mercer of High Desert Church explain it. (*tommercer.com*)

Here's my version of pastor Tom's definition.

> **Oikos** is a Greek word that means *extended household*, which in today's terms would be the 8-15 people in your relational world you currently "do life" with.

Your **oikos** isn't limited to immediate friends and family. It also includes neighbors, co-workers, and even those now-and-then acquaintances who cross your path in a significant way.

If you're still a bit fuzzy on who's in your **oikos**, try asking yourself these questions. *(see Appendix for "Who's in My Oikos?" worksheet)*

Who's in my **oikos**?
- Do I cross paths with her often?
- Do I sense a deeper connection between us?
- Do my words and actions seem to carry weight with her?

The first place I recommend looking for someone to disciple is your very own **oikos**. Who knows, God may have already placed the perfect person right under your nose!

STEP 3: Become a "noticer."

Becoming a **noticer** is one of the most valuable discipleship skills you'll ever develop. In *The Noticer*, Andy Andrews tells the story of a man who changed the course of his whole life, just by "noticing." As you go through your daily routine, put up your spiritual antennae. Pay attention to what people say, what they do, and what they value. Even a brief encounter can reveal a wealth of information, if you know what to look for.

Whenever a younger believer crosses your path, ask her a couple of open-ended questions that leave room for more than a yes or no answer. I'm continually amazed at how much people will share, even with a total stranger, when someone takes the time to ask a question and listen with their heart.

Another helpful kind of noticing is asking around to see if your pastor, women's director, small group leader, or friends know of anyone who's looking for a mentor.

STEP 4: Recognize "mentor-ready."

Mentor-ready is a term I've coined to describe a believer who's ready to become a fully-committed apprentice of Jesus.

Over the years, I've learned *not* to offer to disciple anyone until I witness a sustained hunger to know Christ and learn His ways. While this may sound a bit harsh at first, I've come to believe it's actually a kindness—for both parties.

It's a waste of time and energy
to offer to help someone become
the kind of person they haven't yet decided to be.

It leaves them feeling nagged, and you feeling frustrated.

You don't need to chase someone down to disciple them. Some people need a few more brushes with "reality" before they fully realize the value of becoming a sold-out apprentice of Jesus.

Remember, Jesus let the rich young ruler walk away because he wasn't ready to commit.

We must be willing to do the same.

Then again, I'm not suggesting you callously toss someone aside. Of course, as God leads, continue to love them, engage them in conversation, and pray for them.

But don't offer to officially mentor them until they're mentor-ready!

Mentor-ready believers tend to...

- **Initiate** conversations about Jesus
- **Express** spiritual hunger often
- **Walk in obedience** to what they know so far
- **Show up** for appointments
- **Follow through** on commitments
- **Engage** in authentic give-and-take conversation
- **Enjoy** learning and growing

Familiarizing yourself with these mentor-ready traits will help you to recognize them more easily. *(see Appendix for "Mentor-Ready" checklist)*

STEP 5: Wait for God's green light.

Through trial and error, I've learned that my initial desire to disciple someone is not, in itself, the call to do so. While that heart tug is often the first stage of God's call, it could also be a mere emotional impulse on my part.

For that reason, I've adopted the habit of waiting for the green light of God's peace before saying yes. This means I don't make an offer to disciple someone unless these three things line up.

- She's clearly mentor-ready.
- I sense God nudging me to mentor her.
- I'm confident the time is *now*.

Taking some time to get to know her can make a big difference. It allows you to use your **noticing skills** to observe what she values, her patterns of behavior, and whether your personalities are a good fit.

After you've gone through this process for a week, a couple weeks, or as long as God leads—you're ready to offer to disciple her.

(or if she's super motivated, she may ask you to mentor her!)

Then, no matter how sure you feel, I recommend agreeing to pray about it for a week before making a commitment.

For years, the Holy Spirit has led me to allow this extra week, possibly because I have such a tendency to commit first and count the cost later! Yet experience has taught me to trust this stage of the process.

Nine times out of ten, we both report a "green light" from God. Yet it's that tenth time that makes the week of prayer worth it. Because now and then, I discover that someone who *seems* mentor-ready actually *isn't*. During that week she may remember other priorities, realize her schedule is too full, get distracted, or even lose interest.

Or God may whisper one of these phrases to my heart.

- *You don't have the time or energy right now...*
- *This isn't as good a fit as you think it is...*
- *She's not quite ready...give it some more time...*

I find it difficult to hear those whispers from God in the rush of everyday life. So even if I'm 99.999 percent sure it's a yes, taking that extra week to quiet my heart and wait for God's "green light" has become a trusted safeguard.

ENJOYING THE PROCESS

Now that I've learned to let Him guide the process, it's become quite enjoyable. I've settled into a peaceful rhythm of tuning in, paying attention, and following His lead one step of faith at a time. In a very real sense, He's the one who's doing the choosing. I'm just showing up, being myself, and meeting the wonderful girls He brings my way.

Once you relax and allow God to guide you, it's much easier to recognize those who are truly ready to begin their *disciple sips* journey.

SIP 15

DRAWING OUT
HER GOD STORY

You don't just have a story—
you're a story in the making.
DAN MILLMAN

Come and share a pot of tea.
My home is warm and my friendship's free.
ANONYMOUS

Once you've set **loving limits** and **decided who to disciple**, you're finally ready to schedule your first coffee date!

Before your first meeting, I recommend agreeing on a time, location, and how often you plan to meet. This gives each of you a chance to double-check your availability and make room in your schedule.

Whether you meet in a coffeeshop or restaurant, look for one with a cozy atmosphere and a reasonable degree of privacy. If you meet in your home, choose a comfortable room with the least flow-through traffic so your conversation can remain confidential.

The main purpose of your first meeting is getting to know her better.

And a big part of that is what I call *drawing out her God story*. This is a simple process of asking gentle questions in a give-and-take manner about how she met Jesus, what He's taught her so far, and where He's nudging her toward growth in the future. Being invited into someone's God story is an incredible privilege. It's like being given a front row seat to a miracle in progress!

During this phase, your **noticer** skills will come in handy: *paying attention, pondering, asking, clarifying, and affirming.* Think of it as drawing water from a deep well, one heartfelt question at a time.

GETTING ACQUAINTED
The first step in the drawing-out process is getting to know each other better.

You may want to start by briefly sharing your own heart for discipleship and how you got started. This is a perfect transition to inviting her to share about her own journey with Jesus, including how she became His follower and a brief overview of what He's taught her so far.

Beyond that, if she needs a gentle nudge to get the conversation rolling, you can ask basic questions about her work, family, church connections, or anything else you wish. You can also use this time to refresh your memory on basic information she may have already shared—or fill in gaps in the narrative you haven't heard yet. Keep the tone light and encouraging, and give her answers your full attention.

This "getting acquainted" time can last anywhere from ten minutes to an hour, depending on how God leads.

WADING IN

Once you sense you've established some rapport, that's your cue to move on to the next "beat" in the conversation. Asking one (or both) of these questions is a natural way to nudge the conversation deeper.

So I'm curious, what drew you
to discipleship in the first place?

* * * * * * * * * * * * * * * * * *

What are you hoping to gain
from this spiritual mentoring process?

Her answers will give you a preliminary sketch of where God's working in her life now, and where He's nudging her toward further growth in the future. If she's comfortable with you doing so, I suggest taking a few bullet-point notes as she shares. These details can be a useful guide for setting discipleship goals later.

DIVING DEEPER

Now that you've *gotten acquainted* and *dipped your toe* into discussing motivations and goals, there's one more phase of **drawing out her God story** to complete. It's time to help her dive deeper, drilling down to the bedrock of daily life where transformation is most needed.

You do that by teaching her to *pay attention* to recurring themes and patterns God highlights in her life. *We all have themes in our lives.* Some are positive, like loving to pray or a passion for the underprivileged, while others are more negative, such as a deep sense of inferiority or a tendency to overspend.

The **positive patterns** tend to be areas of growth or gifting God wants to encourage, while the **negative patterns** are areas of sin, doubt, fear, wounding, or weakness He wants to deal with. These often show up as recurring struggles in a given season.

As a new believer, she'll also have gaps in her understanding of how life works in the kingdom. These are areas where her "practical theology" foundation needs to be strengthened with biblical truth.

To help you keep track of the specific areas the Lord highlights, I've created a **MENTORING MILESTONES CHECKLIST**. This checklist includes some common stages of growth new Christians tend to go through on the road to spiritual maturity. They are listed in order from baby believer to mature disciple. *(see Appendix for "Mentoring Milestones" checklist)*

I suggest giving her a copy of the checklist to glance through as you explain themes and patterns. Then give her a few minutes to fill it out.

Pray with her before she starts, to reinforce the habit of inviting the Holy Spirit into the process. After you pray, you may want to leave the room for a few minutes if it's easier for her to concentrate. Once she completes the checklist, take a few minutes to review the results together.

For new believers, almost every area of the mentoring milestones may be needed. For those who've already walked with the Lord a while, some milestones will resonate as gaps while others will be stages of growth they've already passed through.

Keep in mind that neither result is right or wrong. Your purpose here is merely to gain a sense of clarity about where the strengths, blocks, and gaps in her spiritual foundation tend to be. Once a theme or two starts rising to the surface, you both begin to realize, "Wow, that's definitely an area God seems to be highlighting!"

Once you notice this "sizzle" in the air, you know it's time to move on to *Sip 16: Partnering with Christ Together.*

SIP 16

PARTNERING WITH CHRIST TOGETHER

*So the question often is
"Have I accepted Jesus as my Savior?"
But we never ask the question
"Have I accepted Jesus as my teacher?"*
DALLAS WILLARD

*Would you like an adventure now,
or shall we have our tea first?*
PETER PAN

In this chapter, we're getting to the place where the *longing* of her heart meets the *leading* of God.

I assure you, the process described in this chapter isn't complicated. Yet it can be a bit scary at first. In every great adventure, there's a moment of heart-pounding uncertainty as the heroine gathers her courage and decides to act. So if the person you're meeting with feels a bit nervous, that's perfectly normal. *She's learning to step out and trust God in a whole new way.*

At its core, the **partnering with Christ** process is simply learning to *pay attention* and *put into practice* what the Holy Spirit reveals.

That's it.

If you're meeting with a new believer (or feeling a bit nervous yourself) I recommend walking through each of the **mentoring milestone** chapters in the order they're listed. On the other hand, if the person you're meeting with has been a believer for a while, feel free to use them in any order you wish as God leads. Either way, using the principles in this chapter will help you explore each area of growth more deeply.

CATCHING A WAVE

By now, you know what drew her to discipleship and what she's hoping to gain from the process. You also have the results of her **MENTORING MILESTONES CHECKLIST**, which will provide some helpful clues as to what is present or missing in her spiritual foundation.

These are the waves of the Spirit you will catch together.

As you prayerfully discuss her results, patterns and themes will emerge such as...

- *I wish I had more self-control.*
- *I'm not sure how to have a quiet time.*
- *I have trouble relating to God as my Father.*

As you discuss each pattern, God will be faithful to provide conversational clues about where He wants to work in her life. She may mention the same phrase over and over, report feedback from others about a pattern they're noticing, or sense a quickening in her heart whenever a certain subject is mentioned.

With the Holy Spirit as your guide and the mentoring milestones as your *mile markers*, you'll begin to recognize certain areas of growth (or lack thereof) being highlighted. If she draws a blank, try asking one of these simple questions from spiritual growth author, Dallas Willard.

What are You teaching me here, God?

What are You asking me to do?

Or what do You want me to let go of?

What in my heart are You speaking to?

Narrowing it Down

Once you've identified one or more area(s) God is highlighting, write them down or circle them on your existing list. This will be your blueprint for the next few weeks. If there are several areas listed, try and arrange them in the order of priority, based on her felt need.

Then do a brief brainstorming session around how the two of you might practically partner with God in the top one or two areas.

Keep in mind, your goal is to help her **catch a wave of the Spirit** so she can then **partner with Christ** through simple steps of obedience.

Here's a brief review of the process...

- **Ask** the Holy Spirit for guidance
- **Review** her checklist results *(patterns and themes)*
- **Narrow it down** to one or two main areas
- **Brainstorm** practical ways she can partner with God

Now you're ready to *prayerfully agree* on her first set of action steps.

When in doubt, start small.

Don't get tied up in knots over finding the "perfect" action step. Simple movement in the right direction is all that's needed. The Holy Spirit is great at highlighting heart issues and rerouting the process when necessary.

So relax and have fun with it.

Think of your time together as a spiritual growth laboratory where trial and error is not only allowed, but encouraged. If you make a mistake, learn from it. If you're not sure what to do next, ask Him for help. The Master Discipler is more than willing to teach you through every experience.

After a while, a wonderfully relaxed atmosphere begins to emerge. Before long, you're both starting to enjoy the process. After all, what could be more exciting? The two of you get to partner with the King of the Universe as He transforms a life!

Setting Up Scaffolding

Once you've chosen her **action steps** for the next season (or even just the next week), take five or ten minutes to agree on some **spiritual scaffolding** to help the process flow more smoothly.

How often will you meet?
(weekly, bi-weekly, monthly)

Where will you meet?
(home, coffeeshop, restaurant)

When will she do her action steps?
(times per week, by a certain date)

How will you support her or hold her accountable?
(text, email, reminding, encouraging, cheering, praying)

Any other loving limits you need to clarify?
(scheduling boundaries, commitment to meetings, follow-through)

Any other scaffolding she thinks might be helpful?
(may want to re-visit this periodically)

I also recommend choosing a **foundational Scripture** for each discipleship goal you set together. This will help her stay focused on the goal, and provide much-needed inspiration as God's truth transforms her heart and mind.

Wrapping Up

By the end of your first meeting, you will have:

- Put some basic **spiritual scaffolding** in place
- Set one or two **discipleship goals**
- Agreed on **action steps** for each goal
- Chosen a **Scripture** for each goal

It's also a good idea to check in toward the end of the meeting to see how she's feeling about the whole process. While most first meetings are full of excitement and expectation, she also could be feeling a bit overwhelmed. So a simple "How are you doing with all this?" will give you a chance to address any questions or concerns she may have.

And finally, a wonderful habit to get into is closing each meeting in prayer together. This gives the Holy Spirit a chance to seal His work in her life and allows for a sense of closure over all that's been accomplished. It's a helpful way to seal the process of catching a wave of the Spirit together, as you each hear the other speaking directly to God in prayer.

Within a day or two of your first meeting, it also helps to email her a brief bullet-point version of her goals to keep them fresh in her mind.

RIDING THE WAVE

Of course, once you've caught the wave, the next logical step is riding it.

Here are a few tips for spiritual surfing.

- **PUTTING OFF & PUTTING ON**
  Successfully riding each wave will involve *putting off* old ways of thinking and living and *putting on* new kingdom ways of thinking and living instead. It is the practical process of *going from old me to new me* in an area of life.

- **PRINCIPLES VS. METHODS**
  While the *principles* of transformation in Christ are the same for all believers, the *methods* themselves are flexible. Feel free

to use the creativity God gave you to choose methods that work best for you and the person you're partnering with.

- **FULL CIRCLE**
  The two of you will work your way through each God-highlighted area of her life until you *both* agree He's brought it full circle and is nudging you forward.

Your Part

Remember, your primary responsibility is to provide a safe place for her to learn and grow. The actual growth itself is up to God, and of course her willingness to engage in the process.

As you use your **back pocket basics** (GAL MAP), keep these "follow me as I follow Christ" principles in mind.

- **SHARE** truth and **POINT** her to Christ.
- **LIVE OUT** authenticity and obedience in your own life.
- **HONOR** her autonomy and let her make her own decisions.
- **LISTEN** more than you talk—a little advice goes a long way.
- **EMPATHIZE** with her struggles; **CELEBRATE** her victories.

Her Part

Her main responsibility in the discipleship process is **authenticity** and **obedience**. The more honest and obedient she is with the Lord, the more fully she'll be able to ride the waves of transformation in her life.

Encourage her to...

- **ADMIT** honestly what she's thinking and feeling.
- **OWN** her mistakes and **TRUST** God's mercy and grace.
- **RESPOND** to truth and **SOAK IN** God's love.
- **TAKE ACTION** when God tells her to do something.
- **VALUE** honesty, obedience, and intimacy with God.

WATCHING FOR WAVES

It's important to remember that we're not in charge of the waves—God is. While we've been given incredible freedom to choose, the Lord still reserves the right to oversee our spiritual growth, just as a loving father oversees the growth of his children.

So what does He expect us to do while we're waiting for the next wave?

Stay Put

By "stay put" I mean stay in the Word, fellowship, prayer, and daily obedience.

We often look for the "next big thing" from God that will rock our world to its core. While I'm thankful God in His goodness *does* provide thrilling revelations, I'm also reminded of His command to "dwell in the land and cultivate faithfulness" (Psalm 37:31 NASB). And nothing teaches that lesson better than staying put with God during an inexplicable "lull" season now and then.

Stay Delighted

One thing we find especially difficult to do while waiting is to delight. We are natural responders, and waveless seasons (seemingly) give us nothing to delight *in.* Yet God often uses these seasons of calm to re-attune our hearts to the everyday wonders we're usually too frantic to notice.

A good question to ask is...

> *Lord, what blessings do You want to reveal*
> *in this lull season—that I'd probably miss in the waves?*

You may even find it helpful to keep a gratitude journal to remind yourself of what God has *already* given you to delight in. Cultivating the discipline of delight keeps your heart soft and your ears open, so you'll be able to recognize God's voice when the next wave comes.

Stay Alert

When not much seems to be happening, it's easy to become discouraged, distracted—or both. We're tempted to believe God has forgotten us, or even worse, that He knows what's happening but doesn't care.

But as we stay attuned and alert, we often begin to realize that God is still speaking—just much more quietly than He did in the crashing waves. He often uses these in-between times to slow us down, heal us up, change our direction, or provide a much-needed rest. Staying alert to His goodness in lull seasons takes perseverance and practice. Yet His well-placed silence is the perfect preparation for catching the next wave.

My guitar-player husband tells me that the space *between* the notes is every bit as important as the notes themselves. So it is with the voice of God. He knows exactly when to speak and when to remain silent, to best shape the hearts of His beloved children.

Our part is to stay alert, stay faithful, and wait for the next wave.

> Those who wait on the Lord shall renew their strength;
> They shall mount up with wings like eagles,
> They shall run and not be weary,
> They shall walk and not faint.
> ISAIAH 40:31 (NKJV)

LATHER, RINSE, REPEAT

During your time together, you can repeat this process as often as you feel led. Once you're both confident that the current area of growth has come full circle, feel free to move on to the next area of growth God highlights.

If you're not sure what that is, then return to the **drawing out her God story** phase until the Lord reveals the *next* area of growth He wants to work in. Remember, her felt needs and your observations are also part of the "drawing out" process. The steps in *Sips 15-16* can be repeated as often as needed during your mentoring season together.

The purpose of the process is to provide a safe place for her to show up, welcome Jesus into each area of her life, and allow Him to heal and transform her sip by sip—from the inside out.

SIP 17

DISMANTLING THE SCAFFOLDING

To everything there is a season,
a time for every purpose under heaven.
ECCLESIASTES 3:1 (NKJV)

Words imprinted on a giant mug:
"Coffee, because adulting is hard."
ANONYMOUS

Scaffolding is only temporary.

Its purpose is to surround, support, and when it's no longer needed, be dismantled. Yet if a construction project continues long enough, we begin to see the scaffolding as a permanent part of the building, rather than a temporary structure.

This is especially true where spiritual mentoring is concerned. After months or years of meeting together, the arrangement can become so comfortable and cherished that we forget its original purpose: *to help someone build the foundation of her life on Christ so she will be able to fully thrive—and go and make disciples herself!*

I must admit, dismantling the scaffolding isn't always my favorite part. I tend to get emotionally attached, and find myself wishing we could go on meeting regularly for like...ever.

Yet as every mama eagle knows—
if she's done her job well, the eaglets *will* learn to fly!

Still, when your mentee spreads her wings and soars away, even in the best of circumstances, know in advance that a piece of your heart will go with her. Which, as it turns out, is *exactly* how God designed it.

WELCOMING THE DAY

As a spiritual mom, it's important for you to welcome and celebrate the day your spiritual daughter is strong enough, mature enough, and deeply connected with Christ enough to walk to the edge of the nest, spread her wings, and leap toward her God-given destiny.

Once again, your **noticer** skills will come in handy.

Here are a few signs she's getting ready to fly...

- The formerly cozy nest starts to feel uncomfortable.
- She's able to feed herself spiritually.
- She goes directly to Jesus first.
- She needs less flight instruction from you.
- She's discovering her strengths and starting to use them.
- She's scoping out her "next steps" in following Christ.

When these signs start to emerge, there's a pretty good chance that some (or all) of the spiritual scaffolding is about to come down.

BY AGREEMENT

My favorite way for scaffolding to come down is by mutual agreement.

After a year or two, you begin to sense that your season of *official mentoring* may be coming to a close. Whether it's due to internal or external reasons, you both just "know." This is by far the easiest way, because there's no risk of hurt feelings or concern that she may be abandoning the mentoring process prematurely. The scaffolding comes down all at once, yet there's no screeching halt sound effect in the background. Just the contented whir of a healthy, loving relationship that has a very good chance of continuing on a positive note.

If you make it a practice to talk through goals and boundaries periodically, your mentoring relationship will likely end as it began—with mutual submission and respect. There are no guarantees of course, yet in my experience the spiritual scaffolding comes down by mutual agreement about 70 to 80 percent of the time.

GRADUALLY

Another healthy way for scaffolding to come down is piece by piece.

This happens when the bond between mentor and mentee is strong enough to be flexible, and the "letting go" process happens gradually as maturity increases.

While this kind of scaffolding removal is often a joy in the long run, in the short run it tends to happen in fits and starts. I often notice boundaries shifting about three-quarters of the way through the process.

For example, one day you ask a question or make a suggestion in exactly the same way you've done so dozens of times before. And suddenly out of nowhere, there's resistance. She stiffens slightly and says, "Thanks—I'll pray about it." End of discussion. Unspoken message: "Your advice not needed here. I can think for myself."

Not to worry, this is (usually) a sign of growth.

Just as a two-year-old goes through a "do it myself" phase, a young adult often goes through an "if I need your help I'll ask" season of growth. Suddenly any input from you—no matter how releasing or boundary-respecting—feels like a threat to her own emerging process of discovering truth and making her own decisions.

As she struggles to translate her new thoughts and feelings into workable boundaries, she may find it difficult to state her objections graciously, though she honestly doesn't mean to be rude. Other signs that her scaffolding may be shifting include pulling away emotionally, leaving you out of the loop on important decisions, or suggesting that you meet less often.

Before assuming she's upset with you or on the verge of major rebellion, consider this: *She's probably just flexing her wings and needs a bit more elbow room than before.* The truth is, she still needs you in her life—just in a slightly different way.

Now's the perfect time to take a step or two backward and give her the space she needs. This communicates respect and confidence in her ability to make decisions. It also allows you to remain part of the growth process without cramping her style. Honoring this "elbow room" phase improves the chances of your relationship continuing for years to come as mutually encouraging sisters in Christ.

ABRUPTLY

My least favorite way for scaffolding to come down is abruptly—before the mentoring process has been completed.

Imagine tearing down the scaffolding when a building is only half built. This makes it more difficult for construction to continue.

Sometimes scaffolding gets removed abruptly for unavoidable reasons, such as one of you moving to another city or your schedules no longer jiving. But now and then it happens because the mentee isn't willing to continue. While I'm grateful this doesn't happen often, now and then it does. Each time a mentee abandons the process prematurely, whether due to fear of failure, pressure from an unbelieving boyfriend, or a waning interest in spiritual things, it's heartbreaking to watch.

When scaffolding comes down abruptly, it can jar our souls. We wrack our brains for what we could've done differently. We worry about the possible consequences in her life and feel powerless to do anything about it.

Yet it's important to remember that even though she's out of your presence, she's never out of God's Presence. I've seen His full-circle faithfulness enough times to be convinced He's doing everything possible to draw her back to Himself. Yet the choice is still up to her—and that often takes longer than we wish it would.

Some people need to test the boundaries of God's love and wisdom far more than others. At times, the only course left to a spiritual mentor is to lovingly let go, keep praying, and trust God to draw her back. So if one of your mentees abruptly ends things, know that it's not the end of the world. Growth can be messy, and for some this testing phase is a necessary part of the growth process.

Here are some helpful do's and don'ts for trusting God while you wait.

- DON'T worry yourself sick.
- DON'T beat yourself up or fall into condemnation.
- DON'T be afraid to let her struggle, but DO reach out as God leads.
- DO trust God to water the gospel seeds you've planted in her life.
- DO keep praying, entrusting her to God's care.
- DO allow your own heart time to heal, refresh, and refill.

THERE'S NO "RIGHT WAY"
Whether scaffolding comes down all at once, gradually, or even abruptly, don't lose heart. It's not necessarily an indication of failure on your part. After all, even Jesus experienced some pretty abrupt transitions in mentoring relationships—think fleeing disciples, Peter's denials, and the betrayal of Judas. Yet *eventually* His faithful investment paid off, and eleven of the twelve disheartened disciples turned the world upside-down with the gospel!

So gather your courage, refill your cup, and keep following Jesus' example of obeying the Father and investing the gospel—even as you lovingly wait for the occasional prodigal to return.

SIP 18

LAUNCHING AND LISTENING

Throw yourself into this work for Christ.
Pass on what you heard from me...
to reliable leaders who are competent to teach others.
2 TIMOTHY 2:2 (MSG)

Once you wake up and smell the coffee,
it's hard to go back.
FRAN DRESCHER

To be honest, **launching and listening** is the part of mentoring I have the least experience with. Which is why several years ago I realized I needed a better strategy.

It's not that those I discipled weren't being transformed, or even that they weren't affecting their **oikos** for Christ in an as-you-go way. *They were.* But I soon discovered that *encouraging* someone to make disciples was far easier than *equipping* them to actually DO it!

Then I noticed another trend that gave me a clue as to what was happening. Not everyone was growing at the same rate—so while some were ready to start investing in younger believers after only a year or two, others needed to live their way into maturity a while longer before assuming the role of spiritual mentor.

Eventually I began to realize I needed *two* tracks of equipping—one for those who needed as-you-go practice first and another for those who were primed and ready to become official disciplers now.

The idea was to challenge *both* groups to make disciples—
without forcing instant maturity on those who
simply needed more time to grow.

With that in mind, I developed a two-pronged approach to the **launching and listening** phase of discipleship.

COUNTDOWN TO LAUNCH

In either case, once a disciple's spiritual foundation starts to stabilize, you'll notice these qualities begin to characterize her life.

She's increasingly able to...

- ❑ Think of herself as God thinks of her
- ❑ Delight in the Lord and enjoy His company
- ❑ Feed herself spiritually on a regular basis
- ❑ Hear God's voice for herself
- ❑ Recognize lies and take thoughts captive
- ❑ Obey God regularly, without great strain or effort
- ❑ Navigate daily challenges with His help
- ❑ Trust God's strength in her weakness
- ❑ Begin developing a kingdom worldview
- ❑ Live in community with a local church
- ❑ Use her spiritual gifts to serve others

While none of us navigates these areas perfectly, over time a peaceful pattern of what Dallas Willard calls "easy routine obedience" emerges in her life.

LAUNCHING

Once it appears you're nearing the end of your time together, it's time to begin the **launching** phase: *teaching her to make disciples.*

Of course, she's already seen you model the spiritual mentoring process for the past year or two. So now it's time to fill in the underlying principles and give her a chance to practice investing in others while you're still there to encourage and instruct her.

A good way to start is by having her read the last mentoring milestone chapter, *Sip 26: Investing Your Inheritance.* This chapter contains a condensed version of the spiritual mentoring principles found in the *Third Coffee Chat: Encouraging Her Story.* Once she's read the chapter, discuss it together to see if she has any questions. You may also want to discuss any fears she has about the process, and whether she feels comfortable with **as-you-go** or **official mentoring** at this point in her growth.

Then I suggest spending a month or two giving her **small as-you-go mentoring assignments** each week. This gives her a chance to dip her toe into the discipleship pond without getting in over her head. If she finds it difficult to invest in peers, she may want to start with college or high school students, since she's recently passed through those stages of growth herself and may feel more comfortable.

LISTENING

As she practices her **as-you-go** mentoring skills, you will be her *press-enter mentor.* Week by week, she'll share her mentoring experiences with you—what went well, not so well, and anything she has questions about. Just as you have done all along, you will listen, empathize, ask questions, offer feedback, encourage, pray, and help her brainstorm and strategize for the following week.

If she feels overwhelmed, encourage her to take a training step backward and try something easier—like sharing a principle she's learned with a friend or asking a thought-provoking question and listening for the answer. The goal is to help her find conversational ways to practice her back pocket basic skills. *(see e3challenge.net for great as-you-go ideas)*

NOW OR LATER

Some will find this *as-you-go* training plenty for now.

This means she understands the basic principles of how discipleship works and has gained *as-you-go* mastery of engaging others in God-conversations. She's also able to live out her faith with conviction and consistency, and brings the truth of the kingdom with her wherever she goes. Yet she still needs a bit more life experience under her belt before she's ready to become someone's *official* spiritual mentor—especially if they're peers, age-wise.

In this case, encourage her to keep sharing her faith, engaging in God-conversations, and pointing people to Christ in her daily life. You have invested the seeds of the gospel in her heart and mind, and she is an ever-growing disciple of Jesus. Now all she needs is more sun, air, and water (real-life experience) for those seeds to grow into full maturity. As she continues to walk wholeheartedly with Jesus, in due season the harvest will come.

Others will be itching to become *official* disciplers.

If this is the case, praise God!

If she's eager for more, go ahead and walk her through the *Third Coffee Chat* section, chapter by chapter—or maybe the whole book, depending on her level of need or interest.

You may want to extend your mentoring season for three to six months or even a year. Or you could scale back to bi-weekly or monthly check-ins once she starts discipling someone. Again, it all depends on the level of need or interest she expresses to you.

THREE STORIES

Here are three stories of launching and listening I've experienced through the years. While the principles outlined in this chapter will likely be the norm, these stories show that even when the process unfolds a bit differently, the principles of launching and listening still hold true.

Jaimee (self-starter)

As I mentioned before, without any instruction from me, Jaimee often shared the principles she was learning with her friends. Now and then she would even sit them down and teach a principle in detail if she thought it might be of use to them. Amazingly, no one ever took offense because she obviously cared for them and had their best interests at heart.

Bear in mind, none of this was directed by me. She simply couldn't keep all the good things God was teaching her to herself!

Now and then Jaimee would tell me what she'd shared with someone, or ask for advice if she didn't quite know how to help. Soon her friends noticed her life changing for the better, and before I knew it, she was referring them to me for one-off coffee dates or mentoring. She didn't allow her youth or inexperience to hold her back, but started sharing what she *did* know with the people she loved. As a result, the climate of her entire **oikos** began to change.

These "pass it on" moments are a delight, and help keep your heart motivated and encouraged.

Alyssa (as-you-go learner)

Because of her hunger for learning, Alyssa and I have been meeting together for several years (and counting). We share a love for truth and artistic expression and look forward to our monthly God-talks like some people look forward to coffee or chocolate (which by the way, we also enjoy).

Yet somehow, we never quite got to the official "how to mentor" portion of our time together, partly because of the long-term equipping process involved in her calling and partly because I was knee-deep in writing this book.

Yet a year or two ago, Alyssa was asked to be part of her church's mentoring ministry. In addition to her administrative duties, she decided to try her hand at discipling. This was exciting for both of us, and soon she was assigned to a young woman only a couple years younger than herself.

As she shared with me how the process was going, I rarely if ever thought, "oh dear" or felt concern about a choice she'd made. As I listened, it sounded as if she'd already read the how-to sections of this book. But at the time, it hadn't yet been published.

Then it dawned on me: *She's internalized the process over the past few years!* I don't mean to downplay Alyssa's God-given wisdom and insight, which are considerable. Yet I share this experience to encourage you that the very process of *being* discipled is preparation for *making* disciples.

Is there benefit in official training?

Absolutely.

Yet it's reassuring to know that each time you invest in someone, she's getting a glimpse into the heart and "how-to" of discipleship by default!

Katy (on-mission learner)

Sometimes you get to reap the benefit of seeds someone else has sown. In Katy's case, she'd already been discipled during college and was a mature believer by the time she joined the small group I was leading.

She was also a few months away from going on her first missionary journey to India, teaching Math so she could share the gospel on an as-you-go basis. Though I certainly couldn't imagine her needing another mentor, I still felt drawn to get to know her better. Soon we became friends, and when she left for India we did our best to keep in touch.

Soon one year became two, and each time Katy came home on furlough we'd get together for coffee and "download" about India. Each year our relationship grew closer, and soon she was sending me monthly email updates. Without fully realizing it, I had become her *press-enter mentor* for India.

As she shared about teaching, team-building, and all the young people she was officially and unofficially discipling in Jesus' name, I got to know her joys, sorrows, and even her weak spots. Through being invited into the vulnerable parts of her heart, I grew to love and respect Katy even more.

By year three, we had an established pattern of monthly emails and furlough visits until one day she told me she was coming home—for at least a couple years! She felt led to go to grad school, and then see where God was leading her next. Since then, I've had the privilege of being Katy's *press-enter mentor* in person, while she's navigated the transition from a third world country back to the states. I've also been delighted to meet several of her students from India who've come to visit, and seen firsthand how God has used her in their lives.

While I had nothing to do with teaching Katy how to be a discipler, I did have the rare privilege of supporting her as she walked out her calling in India. I now feel a wonderful sense of connection with the kingdom work she did there, as well as some of the people she ministered to, all through the process of launching and listening.

FINISHING AS FRIENDS

One way or another, each season of official mentoring eventually comes to an end. Whether all at once or piece by piece, removing spiritual scaffolding clears the way for a healthy friendship to emerge, whose only bond is mutual love and respect in Christ.

Often the official relationship is only active for a year or two, and then shifts into former-mentor mode. In this case, the mentee is grateful for your help in building her foundation on Christ, and is ready to continue with the Lord without ongoing help from you.

Now and then, the relationship continues long after your season of mentoring ends. In this case, the two of you may continue to spur each other on as apprentices of Jesus for years to come.

Whether your connection continues for a year, two years, or even a lifetime, **dismantling the scaffolding** allows you to close the loop on the current season, and **launching and listening** allows you to send her graciously and lovingly into the next.

CLOSURE CELEBRATION

In the business world, the term "exit interview" may bring to mind images of not-so-fun endings to not-so-favorite jobs.

Yet the heart of a discipleship exit interview is exactly the opposite.

It's a perfect opportunity to reflect, reminisce, and most of all celebrate what God has done in her life during your time together.

(so fun and frivolity are definitely welcome!)

To help set the stage, I suggest reviewing your mentoring milestones checklist at your next-to-last meeting. This will give you a chance to make sure you've met all the mentoring goals God has highlighted during your time together. Plus, remembering how far she's come will help clarify her "next steps" and put you in the mood to celebrate.

If you're both in agreement your goals have been met—it's time to plan the party!

Talk it over and choose something that sounds fun for both of you, whether that means treats, decorations, or meeting someplace special. You may also want to give her a gift to commemorate your time together.

Your celebration day is the perfect occasion to remind her of the changes you've seen in her life and to confer a blessing in whatever way feels natural to you. Feel free to include any specific encouragement God puts on your heart, or even a principle or two you sense may be helpful on her journey.

I suggest ending your time together by praying a blessing over her. She will cherish these words of affirmation from her spiritual mom for years to come, as you send her out with godly confidence and a heartfelt blessing. Rest assured, the spiritual foundation you've helped her establish will continue to make a practical and eternal difference in her life.

WRAP-UP

This completes the **relational how-to section** for encouraging and equipping a younger disciple to become a full-circle apprentice of Jesus. This soul-refreshing process can be repeated over and over, sip by sip, throughout your life.

With each new disciple, you'll discover better ways to follow the Holy Spirit's leading, invest the gospel, and love the person in front of you!

FOURTH COFFEE CHAT

Embracing
God's Story

Mentoring Milestones

Spiritual formation [is] the Spirit-driven process
of forming the inner world of the human self
[so] it becomes like the inner being
of Christ himself.
DALLAS WILLARD

Spiritual transformation
is not a matter of trying harder,
but of training wisely.
JOHN ORTBERG

Mentoring milestones are benchmarks of spiritual growth along the path to maturity in Christ. *Mile markers, if you will.* These milestones represent areas of challenge and growth that have repeatedly risen to the surface in the lives of the young women I've invested in. I pass them along as practical tools to help you embrace growth and track your progress.

HOW THIS SECTION WORKS

Each chapter (or mentoring milestone) introduces a simple *coffee date topic* you can use as a conversation starter. At the end of each chapter you'll find a section called **3 WAYS TO OBEY** which is designed to help you apply each milestone.

PONDER

(thought-provoking questions)

These questions are designed to coax answers from the hidden places of our hearts, where truth sometimes gets stuck. Feel free to use them as pondering, journaling, or discussion *prompts*.

PRACTICE

(sample action steps)

According to Dallas Willard, transformation doesn't come through information alone. We also need the *enzyme* of relationship and the *experience* of putting truth into practice.

PRAY

(a Scripture prayer)

PreScripture is a term pastor Steve Berger coined to describe *a scriptural prescription* for refuting lies and replacing them with truth. Praying Scripture in this way is a powerful tool for renewing our minds and breaking strongholds. *(see "Winning the Mind Wars" sermon series at gracechapel.net)*

USING MENTORING MILESTONES

There's no "right way" to use these milestones, yet here are a couple of the most common.

AS-YOU-GO MENTOR *(as your paths naturally cross)*

Sometimes we're in a season when structured weekly meetings aren't practical. But that doesn't mean you can't invest in the lives of others!

Mentors can use these milestones as **a guide for informal conversations** with friends, coworkers, young adult children, or anyone else they regularly cross paths with.

You don't even have to call yourself a mentor. The simple act of being a friend and asking thought-provoking questions can open the door to spiritual conversation and growth in those who are truly hungry.

This is also a great tool for connecting with those who don't yet know Jesus or are not quite **mentor-ready**. Use these conversation starters to whet the spiritual appetite of those you encounter day to day.

OFFICIAL MENTOR *(weekly, bi-weekly, or monthly)*

A new believer: You can share the milestones with her and work your way through each one together. I'd recommend reading the chapters and doing the exercises in the order they're listed to help her build a solid foundation in Christ the first time around.

---

[1]Pastor Steve Berger of Grace Chapel created the word *PreScripture* and the phrase *PreScripture Prayers.*

A more experienced believer: If someone's been a believer for a while, she may already have internalized some of the basics of the faith. In this case, feel free to pick and choose which milestones to focus on, as the Spirit leads.

SHIFTING FOCUS: For the remaining **mentoring milestones** chapters, I've changed the perspective of the narrative from "here's how you can help *her* grow" to "here's how *you* can grow" so both mentor and mentee can read these chapters together, as needed. *(see Appendix for "Free PDF— 8 Mentoring Milestones" to share Sips 19-26 with mentees)*

Pacing Options

- One chapter a week
- One chapter every two weeks (learn one week, practice the next)
- One chapter a month (to allow time for pondering and practicing)
- Whatever works best for both your schedules

Prep for First Meeting

- Review and absorb the milestones for yourself.
- Keep them in mind as you invest in your disciple.
- Print out **MENTORING MILESTONES CHECKLIST.** *(see Appendix)*
- If appropriate, have her fill out checklist, then review it together.

YOUR OWN MENTOR GAP

As you read through these mentoring milestones with a view to investing in others, you may recognize a gap or two in your own spiritual foundation. You might even find yourself wishing you'd had a chance to process these stages of growth in your own life.

If so, it's not too late!

Here are few ideas for allowing God to fill your mentor gap...

1. Ponder, practice, and pray your way through these milestones privately with the Lord.

2. Ask God to provide a mentor who'd be willing to walk through these milestones with you.

3. You and a friend could *peer mentor* each other—or if several friends would like to participate, you could form a *peer mentoring small group* and work your way through the book together. One of the benefits of this option is it gives you a built-in "posse" of fellow disciplers to cheer you on once you start mentoring!

Whether you walk through these mentoring milestones *before* or *as* you mentor others, you'll never regret allowing God to fill in the holes of your spiritual foundation. Remember, you're His beloved blood-bought daughter, every bit as much as the women He's calling you to invest in.

STARTING THE JOURNEY

Here are the mentoring milestones you'll find in this section. Think of each topic as one tall, grande, or venti-sized conversation!

Sip 19 – A Brand New Identity
Sip 20 – "Mastering" The Daily
Sip 21 – Wish-I-Knew Basics
Sip 22 – Living Like a King's Daughter
Sip 23 – Redeeming Relationships
Sip 24 – Smashing Strongholds
Sip 25 – Your Passionate Purpose
Sip 26 – Investing Your Inheritance

So without further ado, let's get the conversation started!

SIP 19

A BRAND NEW IDENTITY

Anyone who belongs to Christ has become a new person.
The old life is gone; a new life has begun!
2 CORINTHIANS 5:17 (NLT)

After surrendering our lives to Christ, we may look or feel the same. But we are definitely NOT the same. The Bible tells us we're a new creation.

We've been given a clean slate,
a fresh start, and a brand new identity...

This is glorious news. Yet in the beginning, only you and God may recognize the change. (and sometimes, not even you) On planting day, no one rushes up to a farmer and says, "Wow, that's your best crop ever!" Why? Because nothing is visible yet. Only after time, sun, soil, and water have acted upon the seed will it break through its crusty shell and "become" what it already had the full potential to be on day one.

The same is true of our identity in Christ. The seed of the "new you" was planted in your heart the day you said yes to Jesus. Then it's only a matter of time before the sun, soil, and water of growth in Christ make the "new you" visible.

Your new identity will never be based on what people think of you, how many good things you do, or even how much you reeeeeeeeally want to be different. (or even what you think of yourself)

Christ alone is the *source*
of your new identity!

Who He is determines who you are. *And who He says you are is the REAL you.* Once you get that straight, everything else becomes much easier.

ROOTED IN CHRIST

Picture a stunning bouquet of cut flowers with exotic blossoms, lush greenery, and even a few buds that keep opening day by day. Lovely as that bouquet is, here's the sad truth: *The moment those flowers were cut, they were doomed as doomed can be.*

If they're cut off from their roots: They. Will. Die. They're subject to a basic law of nature:

Rooted plants live.
Cut flowers don't.

Before we trusted Christ, our condition was similar. No matter how vibrant we looked on the outside, sin had cut us off from the very life of God. Deep down we sensed we were on a collision course with disaster, because nothing about us was rooted in anything true or lasting. Yet through Christ we've been *grafted back into* the life God always intended for us.

For the first time ever,
our identity is *truly* secure.

Jesus said, "I am the Vine and you are the branches. If a man remains in Me, and I in him, he will bear much fruit. Apart from Me, you can do nothing" (John 15:5).

Always remember that your new identity is connected to the ever-flowing life of Christ Himself. *He alone determines who you are and the glorious potential of who you can become!*

DISCOVERING YOUR IDENTITY

New Family Relationships

The Father, Son, and Holy Spirit have co-existed as a loving Circle of three for all eternity. You might even say they're the perfect family.

While each member of the Trinity is uniquely magnificent in His own right, each one defers to the other two in perfect harmony—even as they play distinctly different roles. The love between the Trinity is so abundant and unending, they created us to share the overflow!

And now that we're grafted into Christ, we are welcomed into that loving Circle—*to experience the boundless love the Father, Son, and Holy Spirit have shared for all eternity.*

**We've been given an *intimate* family relationship
with God the Father, God the Son,
and God the Holy Spirit.**

Before Christ we were distant and far off, but now we're close—we're family. *And this new family identity will last forever.* As you encounter various life challenges, it's important to remember that these three family relationships—Father, Son, and Holy Spirit—are always available to you as part of your new identity.

EMBRACING YOUR IDENTITY

There's a world of difference between intellectually "knowing" you have a new identity in Christ and *deep-down-to-your-toes knowing* you're a new and radically different person with deep roots and an awesome inheritance. For most of us, it takes our mind and habits a while to catch up with what has already happened in our spirit. Here are some suggestions to help you fully inhabit and embrace your new identity.

What You Feed...Grows!

The law of sowing and reaping doesn't only apply to farming. (or consuming mass quantities of Ben & Jerry's ice cream!) Sowing and reaping also applies to how we *think.*

If you feed selfishness or a bad attitude...
that's what grows.

If you feed love, joy, peace, patience, kindness...
that's what grows.

If you feed "I'm a terrible person and no one likes me"...
that's what grows.

If you feed "I'm accepted in the Beloved"...
that's what grows.

"I AM" leads to "I am"

Another way to approach identity renewal is by practicing **if-then** thinking.

If God is my Father and He is love...**then** I'm a beloved daughter.

If I'm a beloved daughter...**then** I'm not rejected.

If I'm not rejected...**then** I'm accepted.

If I'm accepted...**then** I don't have to feel inferior.

If I'm not inferior...**then** I can take that *next step* of faith!

(and so on)

It all begins with an *I AM* statement of who God is, which leads to a corresponding *I am* statement about you. It's a good idea to become familiar with as many *I AM* statements in the Bible as possible, so you can start applying them to your life.

Declarations, Promises, and Descriptions

The Bible contains many other statements about our new identity that aren't stated in *I AM* form—yet they're equally useful in painting a picture of our new identity. Keep an eye out for passages that include God's *declarations* about us, *promises* to us, or *descriptions* of His character and actions. All of these can be immensely helpful in shaping our understanding of who we are in relation to God.

(see Appendix for "Who Am I in Christ?")

GUARDING YOUR IDENTITY

The devil will do everything he can to undermine and attack your perception of who you are in Christ. He knows and fears the power of your blood-bought identity, so he's desperate to distort it, derail it, or make you doubt it. That's why it's so important to stay alert to the enemy's schemes. Remember he has NO authority in your life unless you *give* it to him—by believing and acting on lies.

Here are two of Satan's favorite phrases he will gladly whisper into the heart and mind of *anyone* who's willing to listen. He's used them over and over, from the Garden of Eden onward.

Did God really say...?

God is holding out on you...

The devil is always trying to plant seeds of doubt in your mind regarding who God is, what God said or did, and what God's heart toward you truly is.

Satan whispered these slippery questions to Eve through his slithery forked tongue—and he'll whisper them to you, if you let him. Of course he'll make them *sound* logical and reasonable and relevant, but his *actual* goal is to nudge you toward one (or both) of these two false conclusions.

Come to think of it,
maybe God CAN'T be trusted.

Who needs Him anyway...
I'll just grab what I need for myself.

That's the stance Adam and Eve took, and it led them (quite literally) down the garden path. Yet no matter how believable those lies *feel* in the moment, certain truths remains constant.

1. **God is NOT (nor has He ever been) holding out on you.**
    I Corinthians 2:9; Philippians 1:6; Romans 8:28

2. **God's Word absolutely CAN be trusted.**
    Psalm 33:4; Joshua 21:45; Deuteronomy 7:9

3. **God's NO paves the way to a better YES.**
    (if we're willing to wait for it...)
    2 Corinthians 1:20; Matthew 7:9-11; Galatians 6:9

Standing on the truth of God's Word is one of the best ways to guard your identity. That's what Jesus did during His temptation in the wilderness. He used Scripture to remind Himself of truth and deflect the devil's lies. *And you can do the same thing!*

3 WAYS TO OBEY

PONDER

1. What aspect of your new identity in Christ is most difficult for you to believe and embrace?

2. What experience(s) from the past make it difficult for you to fully inhabit your new identity? Is there any *lie* you've believed about God or yourself?

3. What aspect of your new identity in Christ means the *most* to you? If you could fully embrace your God-given identity in this area, how do you picture your life changing for the better? How can you cooperate with God in allowing that transformation to begin?

PRACTICE

1. **Try giving your new identity a "road test" by putting it into action.**
   Do something this week you would *only* do if you chose to believe God's view of you, rather than your own. (i.e., speaking up for yourself, treating yourself kindly, praying boldly) God is not intimidated when you test-drive His truth. In fact, He welcomes it. "Taste and see that the Lord is good." Psalm 34:8

2. **When we believe lies about ourselves, we tend to become a self-fulfilling prophecy. Why not practice doing the opposite this week?**
   Think of an area where it's tough for you to believe God's view of you. For one week, choose to live as if you *did* believe it. For example, if you find yourself groveling in prayer because you feel unworthy, try starting your prayers with *Thank you God that you delight in me and I'm the apple of your eye.* (Psalm 17:8)

3. **Don't be surprised if conflicting thoughts and emotions surface as you attempt these exercises.**
   Start jotting down your negative "blurts" in brief bullet points as they come to mind, while continuing to practice your new identity. After a week, talk and pray about your "blurts" with a close friend or mentor.

PRAY

Breaking the Stronghold of Mistaken Identity!

As new creatures in Christ, we aren't just remodeled, we're reborn. Yet each day we must choose whether to live life from our new nature or lapse back into living from our old broken one. The more we embrace our new identity in Christ, the more fully we can experience the transformed life He died to give us.

IDENTITY IN CHRIST
PreScripture

Father, I thank You for making me a brand new creature in Christ.	**2 Corinthians 5:17**
I'm grateful beyond words that You've freed me from the law of sin and death, and given me the opportunity to be fully alive again in You.	**Romans 8:2** **Ephesians 2:5**
I now declare my old self dead and crucified with Christ, and fully embrace the new life that Christ Himself lives in and through me.	**Galatians 2:20**
Lord, I refuse to believe the enemy's lies about who You are or who I am in You.	**Genesis 3:1** **Romans 8:31**
I choose to believe Your Word, which tells me I am loved, forgiven, adopted, delighted in, freed from condemnation, gifted by You for the building up of Your church and the spreading of Your kingdom, and destined to rule and reign with You.	**I John 4:10** **Psalm 103:3** **Ephesians 1:5** **Psalm 147:11** **Romans 8:1** **2 Timothy 1:6** **Revelation 20:6**
Thank you for choosing me, Lord, and calling me Your friend.	**Ephesians 1:4** **John 15:15**
Help me to always remember that I belong to You. My name is written in Your Book of Life and engraved on the palms of Your hands.	**Luke 10:20** **Isaiah 49:16**
Now and forevermore, I declare that You and You alone have the authority to say who I am.	**Isaiah 62:2** **John 6:68** **Ephesians 2:13**
And You say I'm a blood-bought, set-free, delighted-in daughter of the Most High God!	**Galatians 5:1** **Psalm 17:8** **2 Corinthians 6:18**

SIP 20

"MASTERING" THE DAILY

Then He said to them all,
"If anyone desires to come after Me,
let him deny himself, and take up
his cross daily, and follow Me."
LUKE 9:23 (NKJV)

Now that we've examined and embraced our new identity, the next question becomes pretty practical. *How do we actually live out this Christ-connected way of life?*

How do we "Master" the daily?

The short answer is start with surrender.

After all, that's how our new life began. We said, "God, I surrender my old broken way of life to make room for the new life You died to give me." So it makes perfect sense that living out our new identity would also involve surrender—a willing choice from a grateful heart to embrace Jesus' ways as our own.

WHY QUIET TIME?

At this point, you may be mentally raising your hand to ask, *Yeah, but if I've already surrendered my life to Jesus, why do I still need a daily quiet time?*

That's actually a great question. Here are a couple simple answers.

1. Because being a disciple is first and foremost a **relationship** with Jesus.

   He doesn't just *tell* us the truth, He *is* the Truth. He doesn't just *show* us the way, He *is* the way. When we signed on as disciples of Jesus, we not only chose Him as our Lord, but also our closest friend and mentor. So there's no other way to learn from Him, live like Him, and become like Him—than to spend actual time in His company.

2. As a car engine needs oil, our hearts and minds need **God's truth and love** flowing through them at all times.

    The great evangelist D. L. Moody was once asked why he talked so much about being refilled with the Holy Spirit. He was quick to answer: "Because I leak."

PRIMING, ABIDING, RE-ABIDING

Have you ever had to pump the handle of a Windex bottle to get the sprayer going? That's how daily time with God works. We've gotta spend some time each day *priming the pump* of God's Word and His Spirit to keep His truth and love flowing through our lives. (otherwise our hearts and minds get "clogged up" with the muck of living in a fallen world)

Here's a three-word reminder to help keep your spiritual well from running dry: *priming, abiding, and re-abiding.*

PRIMING - getting connected

Start the conversation with Jesus...

- Relax in His Presence as you drink your morning coffee.
- Dialogue with Him as you prepare for the day.
- Get the Word and the Spirit flowing through your heart/mind ASAP.
- Priming doesn't take a *lot* of time, but it does take *some* time.

ABIDING - staying connected

He's the Vine, we're the branches...

- Continue in conversation with Him as you go through your day.
- Set prayer reminders on your cell phone.
- Pray deep breath prayers to remind yourself that He's closer than your very breath—and always there with you.
- Wiggle your toes to remind yourself your "roots" are in Him.
- Ask yourself: "Is my spiritual tummy feeling full or empty?"

RE-ABIDING - reconnecting

Repent, reconnect, and re-abide...

Ever find yourself not abiding? If so, don't panic. Just follow **the 3 R's of re-abiding** and you'll be back on track before you know it.

1. **Repent**
    - Agree with God that you've gotten off course.
    - Stop what you're doing and make a U-turn.
    - Head back in God's direction.

2. **Reconnect**
    - Tell God you love Him.
    - Recommit yourself to His ways.
    - Briefly pray / Review Scripture cards or Bible app

3. **Re-Abide**
    - Take the *next* logical step of obedience.
    - Don't overthink it—just do it.
    - Continue abiding.
    - (yep, it's that easy!)

QUIET TIME 101

For those who prefer a bit more detail, here's another analogy for you. In many ways, the process of staying spiritually fit is similar to physical fitness. Feel free to adapt these principles in any way that helps you draw closer to God and walk in obedience to Him.

Spiritual Fitness

WARM-UP: *Starting Each Day with God*

Ideally, your morning time with God is the beginning of an unhurried conversation between you and Him that is meant to continue *throughout the day*. The warm-up is probably the most neglected part of a physical workout. We get in a hurry and forget, or we don't think it's necessary in the first place. Yet without a warm-up, we run the risk of injury or burnout.

We often do the same thing with our spiritual fitness. We rush into our day without connecting with God, hoping against hope that whatever truth and love we have in our spiritual tanks will be enough. Or we try to cram our whole day's conversation with God into one brief period in the early morning. Both approaches shortchange our connection with God and leave us vulnerable to spiritual injury or burnout down the line.

Start your daily spiritual warm-up by finding someplace quiet, being still before God for a few moments, and letting your heart be refreshed by the simple beauty of His Presence.

(even two to five minutes can make a huge difference)

It doesn't take long to pause, take a deep breath, and say *Good morning, Lord. I love you. I can't wait to do this day together...* Once you establish a warm-up routine with God, it can change the tone of your morning—not to mention your whole day.

EATING HEALTHY: *Feeding on Scripture*

God's Word is nourishing to our souls. Feeding on His truth satisfies our deep hunger for meaning and perspective. The Bible is also filled with practical principles for daily living, which provide the nutrients we need to grow strong and healthy. So spending regular time reading, studying, or mediating on God's Word is a *must* for growing disciples.

The good news is, we don't have to spend hours and hours reading the Bible every day to reap the benefits. If you think of the Bible as a huge smorgasbord, it's only common sense that we can't eat everything in one sitting. It's often helpful to start small and work your way up to more intensive Bible study so you don't get discouraged.

Here are a few Bible reading ideas to whet your appetite.

- Choose a book of the Bible and read it in small doses each morning. (examples: John, Philippians, Psalms, or Proverbs) Eating a sensible spiritual meal each morning will go a long way toward energizing your spirit for the day ahead.

- Use a daily devotional app, like *Jesus Calling* or Neil Anderson's *Freedom in Christ*, which both include brief Scripture readings.

- Google verses that apply to your current situation and write them on 3x5 cards—then put them in your purse, take them to work, or tape them to your dashboard or mirror. You may even want to personalize a few verses into your own Scripture prayer to renew your mind in specific areas.

SPIRITUAL CARDIO: *Two-Way Conversation*

Prayer is central to our relationship with God. In fact, it's the very the air we breathe. Yet for many new believers, prayer can be an uncomfortable experience. They tend to feel unworthy, intimidated, or afraid they won't do it quite right—as if everyone else has read the "perfect prayer manual" and they didn't get the memo.

The devil wants to convince you that prayer is difficult, or even impossible. Yet in truth, it's quite simple: *Prayer is a two-way conversation between you and God.*

That's it.

> **You share your heart...and He shares His.**
> **You ask for help...and He answers.**
> **He gives instructions...and you obey.**

Talking with God on a regular basis, frankly and directly, lets Him know you're interested in drawing closer and hearing His voice. Even a few short minutes a day is a great start, especially if that turns into a regular habit.

Yet as important as daily time with God is, our last spiritual fitness habit may be the one that encourages Him to speak to us the most.

WEIGHT LIFTING: *Daily Obedience*

Helpful as spiritual warm-ups are, there's no way you're fitting into your skinny jeans on warm-ups alone! For that you'll need the whole workout.

And the whole workout requires obedience.

You might even call obedience the heavy lifting of the spiritual disciplines. (lifting our "chooser" and moving it forward in faith)

As it turns out, obedience is one of Jesus' favorite subjects. At one point He even said, "If you love Me, you'll obey Me." To some this might seem the teeniest bit legalistic. *After all, I thought Jesus was all about grace and forgiveness, not rules and regulations, right?*

Yet picture this scenario for a moment.

Imagine you have an assistant who hangs on your every word. She follows you around, consults you constantly, and writes down everything you say. Yet when you give her an actual assignment, she rarely takes any steps toward *doing* it!

My guess is, that's how God feels when we pour our enthusiasm into church, Bible study, and even great quiet times, without developing the daily habit of actually *doing* what He tells us to do.

On the flip side, when we make it a priority to *do* what He says, His heart soars with joy. C.S. Lewis's literary mentor George MacDonald once said, "God is easy to please, but hard to satisfy." In the long run, He will never be satisfied with anything less than total transformation. Yet in the short run, even our stumbling steps of obedience bring Him great delight. As Lewis put it, "Every father is pleased at the baby's first attempt to walk:

no father would be satisfied with anything less than a firm, free, manly walk in a grown-up son."

Too much learning and not enough obeying can lead to spiritual bloating, which is the direct *opposite* of the health and spiritual fitness we desire. On the other hand, one of the benefits of acting on God's Word today—is He's much more inclined to teach us *more* tomorrow!

COOL-DOWN: *Thank You / Review*

The other most-neglected part of the workout tends to be the cool-down. Yet it too can pay huge dividends—if we take time to build the habit.

For a while now, God has been whispering to my heart this sing-songy phrase: *Preview-do-review, Preview-do-review.* And gradually, through much trial and error, I'm learning how life-giving this pattern can be. It gives us three chances to partner with God in everything we do—before, during, and after. This is especially true of our daily spiritual fitness.

Here's how it works...

Preview	Morning time with God
Do	Abiding & obeying during the day
Review	Evening overview

The practice of setting aside even five minutes each evening to review the day with God can help you "press enter" on what's happened in the past twenty-four hours: *things that went well, things that didn't, lessons learned, perspective gained, and clarity for applying today's lessons to tomorrow's to-do list.* This gives Jesus a chance to lovingly instruct us without having to chase us down. We just show up every night—or at the end of the workday—and briefly review the day with Him.

After all, how can we learn from our experiences if we never *press enter* on the lessons He's already taught us? And how can we *press enter* on our day if we never pause to ponder it?

A great way to get started each evening is by telling God a thing or two you're thankful for. Philippians 4 says to bring all our needs to Him with thanksgiving. Even if you've had a difficult day, gratitude can help you shift gears, refocus on the good, and renew a sense of godly expectancy.

Once you've renewed your heart with gratitude, briefly review your day with Him. Tell the Lord what went well, what went poorly, and how you felt about it. Then listen for anything He might say to your heart in response. If He gives you any insight or instruction, soak it in and jot it down briefly. Then go to bed. It's that easy!

QUICK OVERVIEW

Once again, here are the building blocks of spiritual fitness we've talked about.

Spiritual Fitness

WARM-UP	Starting Each Day with God	**Psalm 5**
EATING HEALTHY	Feeding on Scripture	**Psalm 34:8**
SPIRITUAL CARDIO	Two-Way Conversation	**Philippians 4:6**
WEIGHT TRAINING	Daily Obedience	**Luke 11:28; James 1:2**
COOL-DOWN	Thanking and Reviewing	**I Thess. 5:18; Ps.119:66**

If you're new to spiritual fitness, I'd recommend starting small. Even fifteen minutes a day can get you on the road to a healthy heart. If that sounds overwhelming, then start with five. (yep, you heard right, *five*)

It's far better to start small and build slowly than to set your goals too high and give up. For now, what's most important is to *decide* on a time, place, and plan for this next week—*and get started!*

THE NEW SORT OF LIFE

To give you one last boost as you begin **"mastering" the daily**, I'll leave you with an encouraging quote from C.S. Lewis.

It comes the very moment you wake up each morning. All your wishes and hopes for the day rush at you like wild animals. And the first job each morning consists simply in shoving them all back; in listening to that other voice, taking that other point of view, letting that other larger, stronger, quieter life come flowing in. And so on, all day. Standing back from all your natural fussings and frettings; coming in out of the wind.

We can only do it for moments at first. But from those moments the new sort of life will be spreading through our system: because we are letting Him work at the right part of us. It is the difference between paint, which is merely laid on the surface, and a dye or stain which soaks right through. [1]

---

[1] C.S. Lewis *Mere Christianity,* Chapter 8: Is Christianity Hard or Easy?

3 WAYS TO OBEY

PONDER

1. **Stationary OR in motion?** Do you enjoy reading, writing, or studying, or do you tend to get antsy when you sit still for long periods? If so, would walking and praying be helpful?

2. **What time is best?** In your current schedule, when's the best time for you to spend some unhurried time with God? (10-15 minutes to start...)

3. **What sort of things tend to break your connection with God during the day?** Example: *Trying to fix things when a problem arises, rather than stopping to ask God for help.* What's your biggest challenge?

PRACTICE

1. **Bible reading.** Experiment with which type of Bible reading works best for you: *traditional, online, or audio*? You may find you prefer one style for reading and another style for more in-depth study.

2. **Prayer.** Consider trying different prayer postures: *sitting down one day, walking and praying the next.* Do you notice any difference in your comfort level, how deep you're able to go with the Lord, etc.? Is one or the other more practical for your circumstances in this season?

3. **Prayer journaling.** Have you ever considered journaling your thoughts to the Lord? Sometimes we find ourselves praying a little deeper when we write our prayers out by hand. If this idea appeals, find yourself a journal and try it for a week. If you enjoy the process, you may even want to give two-way journaling a try. *(see Sip 21 for details—"How We Hear")*

PRAY

Embracing the Habit of Spending Time with God!

In our culture, we highly value self-sufficiency. While personal responsibility and freedom are wonderful values, there's another kind of self-sufficiency that's *not* such a good thing. Like Adam and Eve in the garden, we easily fall prey to Satan's subtle suggestion that we know how to run our lives better than God does. We forget that our new life flows from Christ's sufficiency, and that true freedom comes from yielding our lives to His loving wisdom, strength, and guidance.

"MASTERING" THE DAILY
PreScripture

Lord, like Adam and Eve before me,	**2 Corinthians 11:3**
I acknowledge my tendency to rely	**Genesis 3:1-7**
on my own limited strength and resources	**Jeremiah 2:13**
rather than the abundant supply	**2 Peter 1:3**
of grace, truth, love, wisdom, power, and guidance	**I Corinthians 2:9**
You so freely offer me every day.	
I repent of my stubborn striving and independent attitude,	**Mark 8:34-35**
rather than taking up my cross daily	
and following You as You've commanded.	
Today I surrender my heart to You afresh	**Galatians 2:20**
and choose to seek Your kingdom and Your ways first	**Matthew 6:33**
in all I think, say, and do.	
	Mark 1:35
I commit myself to a regular practice of	**Matthew 14:23**
quieting my heart before You,	**Psalm 46:10, 62:1**
	Isaiah 30:15
spending time in Your Word, pouring out my heart to You,	**Psalm 119:9, 62:8**
listening for Your voice, obeying what You say,	**Habakkuk 2:1-2**
and staying connected with You throughout the day	**John 14:23**
	John 15:5
to the best of my ability.	**Isaiah 30:21**
Thank you that You're faithful to give me	**Galatians 5:22-23**
love, joy, peace, patience, kindness,	**James 1:17**
goodness, faithfulness, gentleness, self-control,	**Psalm 107:9**
and every good thing	
as I learn to walk in Your loving Presence each day.	**Leviticus 26:12**

137

SIP 21

WISH-I-KNEW BASICS

*Christianity has not so much been tried and found wanting,
as it has been found difficult and left untried.*
G. K. CHESTERTON

*One of the lies in our culture today is,
"It's hard to follow Christ." No, it's the easy way!*
DALLAS WILLARD

When we came to Christ, many of us were given clear instruction on salvation, yet little-to-no instruction on how to live out that salvation practically. As a result, we spend many unnecessary years wondering, *Why isn't this faith thing working for me like it does for others?*

Yet Christianity isn't broken—
what's broken is the *way*
we're often trying to live it.

That's a sobering thought.

Yet rather than dwell on the negative, let's focus on the amazing positive.

The way of life Jesus died to give us is alive and well,
and every bit as *life-giving* as it ever was!

This chapter contains some "LEGO building blocks" of spiritual growth I wish I'd known when I first started following Jesus. *Oh, how much wasted time, energy, and effort they would've saved me!*

Maybe you feel the same way? If so, why not end the cycle of frustration by renewing your soul in the basics of the faith? (which is SO much easier than what most of us have been attempting on our own)

When you first read these principles,
they may not sound very spiritual at all—
just simple and down-to-earth.

Exactly!

The Word of God is full of practical principles that help us live out what Jesus taught. When I've applied these truths to my life (or watched others do so), they've resulted in a deeper heart connection with God, increased "traction" with His ways, and a growing sense of peace and power.

You can take it to the bank—God's ways work!

They work because they enable us to *show up* for the transforming work of Christ in our lives, rather than straining and *trying harder* to make growth happen. When you apply these principles, some growth may occur instantly—yet usually it's a gradual process over time. Either way, the Holy Spirit will be faithful to complete what He starts.

All we have to do is keep showing up.

"WISH-I-KNEW" BASICS

HEAR • PRAY
HOW WE HEAR: Simple Steps to Hearing God's Voice
HOW WE PRAY: Speaking Heart to Heart with God

TRUST • OBEY
HOW WE TRUST: Believing God vs. Believing in God
HOW WE OBEY: Loving Obedience Leads to Intimacy

THINK • LIVE
HOW WE THINK: Learning to Take Thoughts Captive
HOW WE LIVE: Learning to Rest in the Easy Yoke

GROW • GIVE
HOW WE GROW: Training vs. Trying in a World of Striving
HOW WE GIVE: The Drink In/Pour Out Cycle

FIGHT • DELIGHT
HOW WE FIGHT: Our God-Given Spiritual Authority
HOW WE DELIGHT: A Gift Wrapped in a Command

Some of these principles have been learned directly from the Lord through my own personal study and experience. Others have been learned from wonderfully wise Bible teachers whose books I read or conferences I attended. Because their teaching has influenced me in such a life-changing way, I consider each one a trusted long-distance mentor. For your information, and their honor, I will list each author in the footnotes. *(also see "Spiritual Growth Reading List" in Appendix)*

Here is a brief overview of the **wish-I-knew** principles.

HEAR

HOW WE HEAR – Simple Steps to Hearing God's Voice [1]

Adam and Eve walked and talked with God in the garden. Jesus said, "My sheep hear My voice." Yet many believers feel insecure about whether or not they can truly hear the voice of God. Any believer can learn to hear God's voice through quieting their heart, focusing on Jesus, and listening for the Holy Spirit. We can also test what we hear through the filter of Scripture and wise feedback from mature believers. God has words of love, instruction, and correction to speak to you—and with a little practice it IS possible for you to hear them.

CORE TRUTHS
Psalm 5:3; John 10:27; Habakkuk 2:1-2; Isaiah 6:8

PRAY

HOW WE PRAY – Speaking Heart to Heart with God

Prayer is an authentic conversation between you and God. Though we often find prayer intimidating, our heavenly Father truly wants to hear from us. David poured out his innermost thoughts to God, and so can we. Try reading a few psalms to get a taste of the gut-level honesty that's possible in prayer. Or personalize the Lord's Prayer or other Bible passages to bolster your courage to pray them for yourself.

CORE TRUTHS
Psalm 42:1-2, 62:8; James 1:5; Romans 8:26; Matthew 7:7; Ephesians 6:18; Philippians 4:6-7; Matthew 6:9-13

TRUST

HOW WE TRUST – Believing God vs. Believing in God [2]

Without realizing it, many of us have gotten into the habit of believing *in* God without truly *believing* His promises apply to us. This allows pockets of doubt to hide in our hearts and sabotage our growth in Christ. Once we recognize and repent of these areas of unbelief, our "traction" with God is restored and we're able to believe Him and rely on His promises more fully.

CORE TRUTHS

Proverbs 3:5-6; Psalm 37:5-6; Isaiah 26:3-4; Psalm 56:3-4; Psalm 112:7; Psalm 27:13; Psalm 40:4; Romans 4:3, 18, 21-24

OBEY

HOW WE OBEY – Loving Obedience Leads to Intimacy

If we're not careful, obedience can turn into a legalistic exercise, rather than an act of love. Sometimes we find ourselves doing what the Bible says merely to avoid negative consequences or to avoid being thought of poorly by other Christians. Yet Jesus repeatedly says: *If you love Me, you will obey Me.* He also says the Father Himself draws closer to those who obey Jesus. Obedience is a matter of the heart. When we obey out of *loving gratitude*, something inside us softens and shifts in God's direction, bonding us more deeply with Him *and* the truth we've just obeyed.

CORE TRUTHS

Luke 6:46; John 14: 15-16, 21; John 15:9-11; John 21:15-17

THINK

HOW WE THINK – Learning to Take Thoughts Captive [3]

Our thoughts are the starting point for our emotions, attitudes, actions, beliefs, character, contentment, and even our state of mental or physical health. Thus, it's only logical the enemy would attack there first. Satan constantly whispers hellish thoughts into our minds, which we often mistake as our own—or worse still, God's. This lulls us into a familiar rut that sabotages our joy and steals our fruitfulness. *The good news is you CAN think differently!* As the gatekeeper of your own mind, you can "arrest" each thought, bring it to Jesus, and receive His life-giving perspective in return.

CORE TRUTHS
Colossians 3:2; Proverbs 4:23, 25; 2 Corinthians 10:5; Luke 6:45; Romans 12:2; I Peter 1:13; Philippians 2:2, 4:8

LIVE

HOW WE LIVE – Learning to Rest in the Easy Yoke [4]
We tend to think of the Christian life as the hard road, and following our own desires as the easy road. *Yet the truth is just the opposite.* While following Christ requires everything of us, it also includes His promise to carry our burdens, empower us by His Spirit, and give us rest. Like a young colt yoked to a more experienced horse, we first must learn to stay yoked to Jesus as He remained yoked to the Father—embracing His will, ways, and pacing for our lives—to experience the rest of "easy yoke."

CORE TRUTHS
Matthew 11:28-30; Hebrews 4:3, 11; Galatians 5:22-25; I Peter 5:5-7

GROW

HOW WE GROW – Training vs. Trying in a World of Striving [5]
Though we come to Jesus through grace, it's easy to slip into trying to grow in our own strength. Soon we're trying hard to be "good Christians" rather than deepening our relationship with Jesus. Yet merely *trying harder* only leads to frustration, legalism, and hopelessness. On the other hand, going into training with Jesus allows His grace into the broken places of our lives so He can *transform* us from the inside out. This often involves taking a training step backward, followed by a smaller step of faith forward, as we learn to lean on His strength rather than our own.

CORE TRUTHS
I Timothy 4:7-8, 6:6; Psalm 1:1-3; Matthew 11:28-30; Romans 12:2; Psalm 51:10; Ezekiel 36:26; Galatians 3:3, 5:25

GIVE

HOW WE GIVE – The Drink In / Pour Out Cycle
As disciples of Jesus we're called to two things: **drinking in** His truth and love and **pouring out** that same truth and love into the lives of others. If we drink in without pouring out, we become bloated and stagnant. If we pour out without drinking in, we become exhausted and burned out. When we practice a healthy balance of both, we're able to experience the *overflowing* kind of life Jesus promised—joyfully giving to others what we regularly receive.

CORE TRUTHS
Psalm 42:1; John 4:14; Luke 6:31, 38; Acts 13:52; Philippians 2:17-18; Acts 20:35

FIGHT

HOW WE FIGHT – Our God-Given Spiritual Authority [6]

Most of us weren't taught how to operate in our spiritual authority—and some of us aren't even sure we have any! Yet once we know who we are in Christ—and learn to recognize lies, resist the devil, wear our spiritual armor, and submit to God—we truly *can* begin overcoming darkness and walking in the authority and freedom Christ died to give us. (and *yes*...that includes you!)

CORE TRUTHS
2 Corinthians 10:3-5; I John 5:4-5; I John 4:4; James 4:7; Ephesians 6:10-12, 13-17

DELIGHT

HOW WE DELIGHT – A Gift Wrapped in a Command

On a tough day, being told to *be thankful* and *rejoice always* can feel a lot like adding insult to injury—after all, what on earth do we have to be thankful about, right? Yet when we *choose* to be truly thankful for even the smallest thing, our body is flooded with feel-good endorphins that improve our mood like a natural painkiller. Not only that, but even a tiny act of thankfulness *weakens* the enemy's grip on our negative emotions and *reconnects* us to God in a tangible way. Like all God's instructions, gratitude truly *is* a gift wrapped in a command.

CORE TRUTHS
I Thessalonians 5:18; Philippians 4:4, 6-7; I Corinthians 15:57; Psalm 118:24; I Chronicles 16:34; Colossians 2:6-7; Proverbs 17:22; Philippians 4:8

[1] Mark and Patti Virkler, *Counseled by God*

[2] Beth Moore, *Believing God*

[3] Joyce Meyer, *Battlefield of the Mind*

[3] Steve Berger, *Winning the Mind Wars* sermon series at *gracechapel.net*

[4] Dallas Willard and John Ortberg, *Living in Christ's Presence*

[5] John Ortberg, *The Life You've Always Wanted*

[6] Keith Martens, *A Field Guide for Followers of Christ*

[6] Neil T. Anderson, *Freedom in Christ* devotional app

3 WAYS TO OBEY

PONDER

1. Which of the **wish-I-knew basics** do you wish you'd known when you first started following Jesus?

2. Which **wish-I-knew basic** do you feel most in need of right now? Spend 5-10 minutes praying or journaling about why that particular "basic" stands out to you, and what you hope God will change in your life as you begin practicing it.

PRACTICE

1. Choose one **wish-I-knew basic** and explore it further, using the resources listed in this chapter or your own research.

2. Practice one **wish-I-knew basic** for a week, and then talk it over with a trusted friend or mentor.

PRAY

Embracing the Basics of Spiritual Growth

Many of us find ourselves "winging it" the best we can, rather than becoming grounded in the basic LEGO building blocks of spiritual growth. This leaves us feeling frustrated and stuck, rather than empowered and free in Christ. Thankfully, God's Word is full of the same grace and truth that secured our redemption, and Jesus is fully able to transform us into His image, one faith-filled step of obedience at a time!

WISH-I-KNEW BASICS
PreScripture

Lord, I'm grateful You haven't left me defenseless, but have equipped me with powerful truths for living my new life in Jesus.	**2 Peter 1:3** **Psalm 19:7**
By Your grace, thank you that I can...	
HEAR Your voice by quieting my heart, paying attention, focusing on Jesus, listening for the Holy Spirit, and testing what I hear by the counsel of Your Word.	**John 10:27** **Habakkuk 2:1-2** **2 Timothy 3:16**
PRAY to You any time of the day or night, pouring out my concerns to You, as well as my thanksgiving and praise, knowing You will hear, answer, and even help me to pray.	**I Thessalonians 5:17** **Philippians 4:6-7** **Romans 8:26**
TRUST You in all circumstances, regardless of how I feel, knowing that You will keep Your promises to me, just as You kept Your promises to all those in the Bible who trusted You.	**Psalm 62:8** **Romans 4:3, 18** **Hebrews 11**
OBEY You from my heart, not to earn Your love, but out of deep love and gratitude for all You've done for me. Thank you that as I obey, it draws me closer to You.	**John 14:15, 23**
THINK the way You want me to, by bringing each troubling, discouraging, or doubtful thought to You, and receiving Your life-giving perspective in return.	**2 Corinthians 10:5** **Philippians 4:8** **I Corinthians 2:16**
LIVE in the "easy yoke" with Jesus, allowing Him to free me from legalism, lighten my load, teach me to keep in step with Him, and empower me by the Holy Spirit.	**Matthew 11:28-30** **Galatians 5:25**
GROW as an apprentice of Jesus, being trained by Him and transformed from the inside out, instead of trying harder to be a "good Christian" in my own strength.	**I Timothy 4:7**
GIVE and receive Your truth and love in a healthy way, drinking in Your Word, Presence, and fellowship with believers and pouring out by helping others learn to do the same.	**John 4:14, 7:38**
FIGHT spiritual battles boldly, using my biblical authority in Christ to expose lies, extinguish the devil's fiery darts, and move forward confidently in the truth.	**I John 4:4, 5:4-5** **2 Corinthians 10:3-5** **James 4:7, 2 Timothy 1:7** **Ephesians 6:10-11**
DELIGHT in Your blessings, on good days and bad, by embracing gratitude, Your gift to me wrapped in a command, which reconnects me with Your goodness.	**I Thessalonians 5:17-18** **Philippians 4:4, 6-9**

SIP 22

LIVING LIKE
A KING'S DAUGHTER

*See what great love the Father has lavished on us,
that we should be called children of God!
And that is what we are!*
I JOHN 3:1

*Do not be afraid...for your Father
has been pleased to give you the kingdom.*
LUKE 12:32

As the deep-down truth of who you are in Christ becomes more real to you, a peaceful sense of dignity starts to permeate your daily life.

Things you once tolerated begin to feel uncomfortable. Slightly fuzzy truths start coming into focus. Before long you're holding your head higher and walking with more confidence than you ever imagined possible.

**You're learning to shed that old identity
and *embrace* the new you...**

YOUR ABBA'S HEART

As your Heavenly Father's treasured daughter, you are the absolute apple of His eye. By earthly standards, this may sound too good to be true. It's quite possible you never felt protected by your earthly father, or your relationships with men have left you feeling anything but cherished.

But the following passages read so much like a love letter, they're difficult to ignore.

I will call...her who was not beloved, "beloved."
ROMANS 9:25 (NKJV)

*He brought me out into a spacious place;
he rescued me because he delighted in me.*
2 SAMUEL 22:20

147

Keep me as the apple of your eye;
hide me in the shadow of your wings.
PSALM 17:8

The King's daughter is all glorious within.
PSALM 45:13 (NASB)

While it may take some time for your heart to *feel* God's fatherly love as deeply as you'd like, the unmistakable *fact* remains.

You are a much-beloved daughter of the King of Kings!

QUEENLY BOUNDARIES

Over the years, I've noticed that many women enter adulthood with little to no awareness of their need for personal boundaries. This leaves them walking through life unprotected—without even fully realizing it.

That's where the perspective of a spiritual mentor can be extremely helpful. Allowing someone you trust to hold up a loving mirror helps you gain clarity on where you may be leaving yourself open to disrespect, mistreatment, or even abuse. Talking about these issues with a mentor also provides a safe environment for considering and choosing boundaries that reflect your true identity as a daughter of the King (Proverbs 3:13, 19:20).

Here are three common boundaries you may want to discuss with someone you trust.

My Lady's Modesty

As a daughter of the King, part of your birthright is to carry yourself with grace and dignity. Yet after years of being surrounded by ever-shifting standards, it's easy to lose sight of what grace and dignity even *look* like.

A few years ago, I discipled a young woman whose tenderhearted love for Jesus was evident to all who knew her. Yet week after week, she showed up at my house wearing increasingly sexy outfits that seemed out of place with her ever-deepening faith. I knew I needed to address this, but found myself putting off the conversation because I didn't want her to feel judged or attacked.

So I asked God for wisdom and waited.

About three weeks later she showed up wearing an even more plunging neckline than usual, and I realized the time to speak had finally arrived.

I shot up one last "help me, Jesus" prayer and dove in.

"You know, I've been noticing that some of your outfits are a bit revealing, and I was wondering...have you ever considered how the way you dress represents Jesus?"

I waited in silence as she pondered the question.

When she finally answered, I couldn't have been more surprised.

"Wooooow, that is so true—I never thought of it that way. No, that's definitely *not* how I wanna represent Jesus. Thank you so much for bringing this to my attention!"

What a huge relief. I didn't have to embarrass her or make a big deal of it. All I had to do was gently bring up the subject, and God took it from there.

In the weeks that followed, her wardrobe choices began to shift in the direction of stylishly elegant yet modest. More and more, she looked on the outside like her heart already looked on the inside.

Mind you, I gave her no dress code.

All I did was gingerly ask, "Hey, have you ever considered...?"

And God did the rest.

While there's no guarantee you'll always receive such a positive response, I will tell you this. When someone truly knows you love her, your voice in her ear is a lot louder—*even if you whisper.*

If you ever need to have the "modesty talk" with someone, here are a few thoughts to help get you started.

Modesty matters because it...

- *Expresses* dignity
- *Preserves* purity
- *Protects* personal boundaries
- *Preserves* intimacy

CORE TRUTHS: I Timothy 2:9-10; I Peter 3:3-5

Friendship Firewalls

I daresay the term *friend* has changed more in the past decade than in all of human history. Thanks to the Internet, you can now be "friends" with someone you know very little about—including whether or not they actually *are* who they say they are!

Plus, many people use social media as an online journal for their personal thoughts, feelings (and location) without any sort of safety screening process in place. This exposes the personal details of their life to virtual strangers, simply because they happen to be "friends" on social media.

While sharing your life with a trusted circle of friends is healthy, this kind of unfiltered sharing can be very dangerous. It reminds me of Jesus' analogy about the folly of giving precious things to those who can't appreciate them (Matthew 7:6). Not only could your feelings get hurt, but opening your life to those who haven't proved themselves faithful could also have serious relational (and safety) consequences.

If you're not sure whether your **friendship firewalls** are healthy, here are a few questions to prayerfully discuss with a friend or mentor.

- Do I tend to let people in too quickly?

- How do I currently tell the difference between an acquaintance and a close friend? How would a person *earn* a slot in my inner circle?

- If I were using an online dating site, how would I decide who was safe and who wasn't?

People are hungrier than ever for authentic connection. Yet often their relational plate is piled so high with unsatisfying or even dangerous friendships, they're on the verge of relational malnutrition—without even realizing it.

Here are a few bricks to help you build your friendship firewall.

A close friend is someone who...

- I've known for a while (think years...not days or weeks)
- I've met in person (when possible)
- Other people I trust have met (or interacted with)
- Treats me with dignity and respect
- Has proven themselves worthy of my trust
- I feel safe to share deeply with

If you'd like to read more on the subject, here are some books I recommend.

- *Safe People* (Henry Cloud & John Townsend)
- *Boundaries* (Henry Cloud & John Townsend)

CORE TRUTHS: I Corinthians 15:33; Proverbs 12:26, 13:20, 18:24, 22:24-25, 27:5-6; I John 4:1

Flirting with Danger

The next logical area of boundaries, and the one I feel the deepest concern about, is romantic relationships.

As a natural outgrowth of a lack of identity, modesty, and friendship filters, it makes sense that many women in their twenties and thirties struggle with a lack of healthy boundaries with the opposite sex.

There are many reasons why this cultural drift has occurred, but the sad bottom line is this: *Where dating is concerned, Christian young women are more likely to go with the flow of culture than with the flow of the church.*

That said, there are still plenty of opportunities to lovingly encourage women to consider their dating boundaries in light of their relationship with Christ. (we'll talk more about that in *Sip 23: Redeeming Relationships*)

For now, here are a few thoughts worth discussing with a friend or mentor.

- Are my current dating boundaries more in line with Scripture or culture?
- Have I been flirting with danger in my interactions with men without even realizing it?
- Are there any personal boundaries I sense God leading me to change, or set for the first time?
- Whether I'm currently in a romantic relationship or not, what steps could I take to build healthier boundaries for the future?

Ways to set queenly boundaries...

- Dress stylishly yet modestly.
- Be wise about who I share my time and heart with.
- Prioritize my connection with fellow believers.
- Pace my depth of sharing with the commitment level of relationship.
- Treat my body like a temple of the Holy Spirit.
- Make a renewed commitment to sexual purity.
- Decide to save sex for marriage. *(it IS possible—and beneficial!)*

You might also want to check out this helpful book.

- *Boundaries in Dating* (Henry Cloud and John Townsend)

CORE TRUTHS: 2 Timothy 2:22; 2 Corinthians 6:14, 15:33; Song of Solomon 2:7; I Thessalonians 4:3-5; Ephesians 5:3; I Corinthians 6:18;

Proverbs 19:2, 31:30, Proverbs 4:23; I Corinthians 10:31; Matthew 6:33; Jeremiah 29:11

PRINCELY PROSPECTS

Once you truly see yourself as a king's daughter and start setting queenly boundaries, something deep inside begins to change. Soon you're thinking, choosing, and even carrying yourself differently. And as you ponder your dating life, you may develop what I call *princely expectations.*

Character Counts

If you watch the latest commercial or sitcom, the conclusion seems to be that if a guy is rich, talented, or good-looking enough, he can treat you any old way he wants. Sadly, many women have bought into the idea that "men are men" and "boys will be boys" and "women just have to put up with it."

Yet once you get to know Christ, you discover there IS one man in your life who treats you with queenly dignity and respect. And suddenly you find yourself looking for an earthly husband whose character reminds you of Jesus.

- ❏ Does God come first in His life?
- ❏ Is he someone who keeps his word?
- ❏ Does he live by godly principles, quite apart from me?
- ❏ Is he someone who builds me up? (or tears me down...)
- ❏ Do I find myself closer to God when I spend time with him?
- ❏ Is he the kind of man a daughter of the King would date?

If you can answer "yes" to these kinds of questions, he's just passed the character test.

Be Careful Little Eyes

Apparently, the old Sunday School song got it right: *Be careful little eyes what you see.*

One of the heartbreaking aspects of our cyber culture is the 24/7 availability of pornography. This has had a devastating effect on millennial relationships. *Yet as a daughter of the Most High God, it is still entirely reasonable to expect your man to only have eyes for you.*

While we've all heard that men are visual creatures, it does NOT mean that men are slaves to their eyes. On the contrary, it means they must learn to *focus* their God-given impulses in a healthy way.

One thing to keep an eye out for is a guy who can't seem to keep *his* eyes on you, even when you're out together in public. If he can't keep his eyes off other women while you're dating, imagine how lonely you're gonna feel once you're married. *This is a warning sign from God to run, run, run!*

CORE TRUTHS: Matthew 5:28; Job 31:1; I John 2:16; James 1:13-15; Galatians 5:16, 24, Ephesians 4:22; Colossians 3:5; I Thessalonians 4:4-5; 2 Timothy 2:22; Proverbs 9:14-18; Proverbs 5:15-20; Hebrews 13:4

The Company He Keeps

Another thing to pay attention to is: *What sort of people does he hang out with?*

When you're first gaga over someone, this question can sound insignificant. Yet a year or two later, you may find yourself wishing you'd asked it.

Here are a few more specifics it couldn't hurt to ask—but it could hurt plenty *not* to ask.

- ❑ Does he spend social time with other believers or mostly hang out with non-Christians?
- ❑ What sort of things do they do when they get together?
- ❑ Do his friends know him well, or is he more of a loner?
- ❑ Is there anyone in his life he's accountable to?
- ❑ Do I admire his friends or find them immature?
- ❑ Does he show any interest in getting to know my friends?
- ❑ Does he have a healthy relationship with his family?
- ❑ Would I feel proud to introduce him to my family?

While getting to know someone one-on-one is valuable, spending time with them in a group gives you the chance to see a whole other side. It's the difference between them *telling* you what kind of person they are, and *seeing* it for yourself.

Being a daughter of the King entitles you to a life of beauty, dignity, and grace. The more you learn to know your Father's heart, set queenly boundaries, and expect princely prospects, *the more fully you'll find yourself living—and feeling—like a king's daughter!*

CORE TRUTHS: I Corinthians 15:33; Proverbs 4:23, 13:20; Genesis 2:18a; I John 3:18

3 WAYS TO OBEY

PONDER

1. **Do you find it easy or difficult to picture yourself as a beloved daughter of the King?** If it's difficult to think of yourself that way, what kind of thoughts come to mind instead?

2. **Where do you think those negative thoughts about yourself came from?** How do you think God's view of you might differ from your own?

3. **It stands to reason that a new identity would bring a new lifestyle.** What boundary or lifestyle changes do you think would help you live more in harmony with your new identity as a daughter of the King?

PRACTICE

1. **Google verses about God the Father and choose four of your favorites.** Write them down on 3 x 5 cards and meditate on one per week for a month.

2. **Research one woman in the Bible who exemplifies the kind of woman you'd like to be.** Why do you feel drawn to her story and what about her reflects the legacy of being a king's daughter?

3. **If you're in the mood for a bit of whimsy, buy yourself an inexpensive crown or tiara from a party store as a reminder of who you *truly* are.** I once saw an elderly woman put on a tiara, and she morphed into a five-year-old princess before my very eyes!

PRAY

Learning to Think and Live Like a Beloved Daughter!

For one reason or another, many women find it difficult to think of God as their Father, or themselves as His beloved daughter. Yet knowing you are a chosen member of God's royal family is central to developing healthy boundaries and expectations for your life—because being His beloved daughter gives you dignity, value, purpose, and hope!

KING'S DAUGHTER
PreScripture

Father God, thank you for loving me, giving me a new identity as Your daughter, and embracing me as part of Your forever family.	Galatians 3:26 Luke 12:32
As I learn to embrace my new identity in You, help me understand and embrace the new boundaries and expectations that makes possible.	I Corinthians 2:9 2 Corinthians 5:20
In areas I never knew I needed boundaries, please open my eyes and ears to the protection they offer and teach me to set them firmly, kindly, and wisely.	I Timothy 2:9-10 Proverbs 14:15 James 1:5
In areas I never realized I had the right to say "no" please give me the courage to speak up for myself and the strength not to waiver if my "no" is challenged.	Matthew 5:37
When I find it difficult to hope for more, please help me to trust You for the kind of life You've had in mind for me all along, and give me the courage and persistence to take baby steps of faith in that direction.	I Corinthians 2:9 John 10:10b Proverbs 13:12 Luke 17:5-6 Zechariah 4:10
And in areas where I've never felt good enough or strong or important or valuable enough to be the kind of person I deep down long to be, please renew my vision of what is possible for a beloved daughter of the Most High God.	Psalm 45:13 Isaiah 43:1 Romans 8:16-17 Psalm 27:13-14
May I be a living breathing example of the beauty, grace, truth, purity, strength, and redemptive love of my beloved Father's kingdom!	Colossians 3:17 John 15:8 Colossians 1:27

SIP 23

REDEEMING RELATIONSHIPS

Beloved, if God so loved us,
we also ought to love one another
I JOHN 4:11 (ESV)

Since our new identity springs from our relationship with Christ, it's only logical that His transformation process would spill over into our human relationships. In this chapter, we'll briefly explore the kinds of *relational shifts* that tend to occur during discipleship.

ARE YOU MY MOTHER?
Helping to Heal the Mother Wound

One relational issue you may encounter is what psychologists call "the mother wound." The fact that there's an actual term for it reveals that mother-daughter trauma is more common than we think.

Motherhood is one of God's most wonderful inventions, and most of us have received incredible love and sacrifice from our moms. Yet for some, the much-needed experience of emotional nurturing doesn't get passed down from mother to daughter, often because the mom herself didn't receive it growing up.

When emotional nurture is missing from a mother-daughter relationship, the daughter tends to interpret the lack of connection as a negative statement about her own value or lovability. She may even carry a deep sense of rejection into other relationships and find herself consciously or unconsciously trying to fill that sense of loneliness in her own heart.

Like the baby bird in the children's classic *Are You My Mother?*, a daughter may seek out person after person in hopes of finding the kind of nurture and support her soul longs for.

Or she may respond exactly the opposite, by shutting down her emotions and shying away from anything remotely resembling vulnerability.

God often uses spiritual mentoring
to heal mother wounds.

The mentoring process provides a natural opportunity for a young woman to be heard, affirmed, encouraged, and delighted in by someone of her mom's generation.

The goal is never to replace the mentee's mother, but to make room for God to provide the emotional nurturance a daughter may have missed for one reason or another. She can learn to allow God to fill her emotional well, whether or not her own mom ever learns to do so. This often enables her to understand, forgive, and love her mother more deeply.

It's a beautiful thing to watch God fill our mentor and mother gaps, as He graciously brings people together in the body of Christ.

PSALM 68:6 *God sets the lonely in families, he leads out the prisoners with singing.*

DADDY'S LITTLE GIRL
Restoring Faith in Father God

There's a special relationship between dads and daughters.

At least that's how God intended it to be.

Unfortunately, brokenness between fathers and daughters is far more common than we'd like to think. If a daughter's relationship with her father has been disappointing or deeply hurtful, she tends to transfer that hurt and disappointment onto herself and God, often without realizing it.

Restoring faith in Father God is essential
to learning to walk in trusting obedience.

A mentoring relationship may be the first place a young woman has been able to honestly admit her feelings or pause to consider how her relationship with her father may have affected her view of God.

For some, finding the courage to share with a trusted friend or mentor is all that's needed to expose the enemy's lies and start replacing them with truth. Others may need the loving nurturance of a friend, mentor, or professional counselor over an extended period to renew their confidence in a tenderhearted Heavenly Father whose "hope does not disappoint" (Romans 5:5).

At times, it may be helpful for a married mentor to invite a mentee over to spend time with her family. Seeing firsthand how a godly man interacts with his wife and kids can be incredibly healing for someone who's never witnessed this kind of respectful love in action.

Yet even the best human father is only a pale reflection of our Father God, who has never missed a moment of our lives or forgotten a single promise. He's never ignored us, abused us, or failed to act on our behalf. Even if your earthly father has failed you, your *Abba* never will.

As you gradually learn to trust the constancy of God's love, you will become more and more free to forgive and accept your earthly father for who he truly is, rather than the all-powerful figure he appeared to be when you were a child.

This doesn't mean your father-daughter relationship becomes instantly perfect, but it *does* mean you can allow him to be human, while you learn to rely on your Heavenly Father's abundance, rather than being controlled or embittered by the past.

As we transfer our parental expectations to our Heavenly Father, we are freed up to honor our earthly fathers in a more realistic way.

ROMANS 8:15 (ESV) *For you did not receive the spirit of slavery to fall back into fear, but you have received the Spirit of adoption as [daughters], by whom we cry, "Abba! Father!"*

ROMANTIC RELATIONSHIPS
Dangerous Curves Ahead!

When a young woman I'm mentoring announces she's got a new guy in her life, I fasten my seatbelt and pray a little prayer: "Oh Lord...heeeeeeeeeeeere we go!"

Because in my experience, dating can be risky business for a new disciple-in-training. Nothing has as much potential to hinder a woman's spiritual growth as a romantic relationship gone awry. After seeing this pattern repeated so many times, I found myself wondering why.

Then a few years back, I tried two different kinds of cell phone cases— *drop-proof* and *waterproof*. And suddenly the whole scenario made a *lot* more sense.

A *drop-proof* case does a great job of protecting the phone from all sorts of external dangers. It's constructed of a super durable layer of plastic that's insulated by a softer layer of rubber, both of which combine to make your phone drop proof, shock proof, kick proof, and practically run-it-over-with-a-truck proof.

On the other hand, the *waterproof* case doesn't look nearly as sturdy. Its main claim to fame is you can completely submerge it without causing water damage. But there's one catch: *Before you put the phone in the case, you've gotta submerge it underwater to test for hairline fractures!*

I've attempted this procedure myself—and believe me it's *beyond* tedious. Yet as anyone who's ever dropped her phone in the gutter can tell you (or heaven forbid, a bathroom fixture), it's well worth the trouble to make sure the case is completely watertight!

The *drop-proof* case reminds me of most believers. In many instances, they're strong and steady in their faith, and have learned to withstand blows from the outside world with a fairly high level of resilience. Because of this, it's tough for them to imagine anything shaking their faith, since they're able to withstand being dropped, kicked, or even run over without losing heart.

But then they get into a romantic relationship. And suddenly they're submerged in all sorts of thoughts, feelings, hopes, dreams, fears, insecurities, and hormonal responses they haven't experienced for a long time—if ever. *And before long, their heart springs a leak.* The next thing you know, their whole life is taking on water. And they're more surprised than anyone—because after all, they were *drop proof*, right?

I don't share this analogy to discourage you. I share it in hope that you'll take steps to *prevent* this sort of tidal-wave-of-the-heart from engulfing your life—or the life of someone you care about.

The best relational waterproofing
I know is discipleship!

When we allow God to reveal and heal the hairline fractures in our spiritual foundation *before* a relationship starts, this kind of relational crash (and subsequent sinking!) can often be avoided—or at least downgraded to a slight fender-bender.

Yet for that to happen, we've gotta be willing to submerge our hearts in truth and godly vulnerability long enough for the *waterproofing* process to do its preventive work.

This may involve allowing God (and a trusted mentor or counselor) into the tender places of your heart where emotional fractures develop, so healing can take place. It may also include brainstorming a few dating scenarios with your mentor *before* you start a relationship, so you can make a few **pre-decisions** about your **dating boundaries**.

While avoiding all emotional pain isn't possible, inviting a trusted friend or mentor to help you navigate the dating process gives you a much better chance of enjoying the ride and reaching your desired destination: *a mutual, Christ-centered partnership with someone you're crazy about!*

PROVERBS 1:7 *The fear of the Lord is the beginning of knowledge, but fools despise wisdom and instruction.*

DIFFICULT PEOPLE
Drawing from the "Loving Well"

In the world's system, you basically love those who love you back. While you might make an exception now and then, as a rule it's pretty much "you scratch my back and I'll scratch yours." And, of course, there's the unspoken corollary: "If you mess with me, you'll live to regret it!"

But in the kingdom of God, things work a bit differently. Jesus calls us to love the unlovely, go two miles when we're asked to go one, and forgive those who mistreat us. *But how do we do that?*

Beth Moore teaches a brief-yet-practical study called *Loving Well* that describes four different kinds of people we are called to love—*joy, testy, far, and foe.* The premise of the study is that none of us have what it takes to love others well in our own strength—especially those we find difficult to love. *(see Appendix for "Spiritual Growth Reading List" – Relationships)*

> **To love others well, including ourselves,**
> **we must learn to draw from God's "loving well"**
> **rather than our own limited resources.**

This shift in focus allows God to pour *His* love for that person into our hearts, changing our perspective and empowering us to love even the most "prickly" people in our lives.

Plus, when we find it difficult to love others, it often means we're running a quart low ourselves, which means it's time to dip into the "loving well" of God's heart for us.

This new way of loving takes practice, and at times it may even feel impossible. Yet gradually, you'll find it grows easier to take a deep breath, dip into God's perspective, and receive His power to love the person in front of you.

(even that girl looking back at you in the mirror...)

PSALM 133:1 *How good and pleasant it is when God's people live together in unity!*

3 WAYS TO OBEY

PONDER

1. **Has something painful or disappointing in my relationship with my mom or dad negatively affected my relationship with God?** Is it possible I may have misjudged God's heart toward me? What is the lie I've been believing about Him—and the corresponding truth I need to replace it with?

2. **Do my boundaries with the opposite sex reflect my identity as a daughter of the King?** If not, what are some changes I could make in the way I approach dating, interact with the opposite sex, treat my significant other, or allow him to treat me?

3. **Is there anyone in my life I find difficult to see through God's eyes?** What's a practical way I can dip into "the loving well" to love them with God's love instead of mine?

PRACTICE

1. **Do I need to forgive either of my parents for wrongs done or affirmation or nurture omitted?** Consider writing a "for your eyes only" letter to God OR one or both of your parents to help sort out any hurts, disappointments, or injuries you experienced. When it's finished, read the letter out loud, forgiving your parent(s), surrendering the situation to God, and trusting Him to bring things full circle as He sees fit.

2. **Write out a contract between you and God for how you'll choose to conduct yourself with the opposite sex**—for the sake of purity and fully inhabiting your dignity as a king's daughter. Then sign and date it and declare out loud: "I am a daughter of the Most High God... I am worthy of *love, respect,* and *definitely* worth waiting for!"

3. **Who could I practice loving from God's "loving well" today?** Examples: cashier, customer service rep, or friend/family member who's on your last nerve.

PRAY

Allowing God to Redeem Your Relationships!

Since our whole new life *began* with a relationship with Jesus, it only makes sense that every other relationship in our life would also be affected. Relationships in the kingdom of God work differently than they do in the world, which can take some getting used to. It's perfectly normal to go through an adjustment period of learning to navigate each kind of relationship differently than we did before we met Christ.

RELATIONSHIPS
PreScripture

Lord, thank you for choosing to redeem my life through relationship with You.	John 14:6 John 7:38
Thank you for the bond of truth and love that exists between Your heart and mine. Teach me to allow that same truth and love to flow through me to others.	John 15:13, 15 2 Corinthians 1:3-5 Psalm 133:1
Help me to treat others kindly, listen before I speak, have wise boundaries, and live at peace with others as far as it depends on me.	Proverbs 31:26 James 1:19 Matthew 5:7 Romans 12:18
When I have wounded others, help me to empathize, ask forgiveness, and take responsibility to change with Your help.	Matthew 5:23-24
When others hurt me, help me forgive them and trust You to heal my heart.	Matthew 6:14-15 Psalm 34:18
When others misunderstand me, help me run to You first, as the One who knows me best, inside and out.	Psalm 55:12-14 Psalm 139:1-6
If my parents let me down, help me trust You to put things right and re-parent me where they cannot.	Psalm 27:10-11 Isaiah 49:15-16
Where romantic relationships have wounded me, be my Comforter, Healer, and Provider, and help me grow in wisdom through the pain.	Psalm 147:3 Isaiah 54:5 Proverbs 9:9
When loving others stretches me to my limit, help me draw from Your "loving well" so I can see them from Your perspective and love them with Your love.	John 15:12 Matthew 5:46-47 I John 4:7

SIP 24

SMASHING STRONGHOLDS

The weapons we fight with
are not the weapons of the world.
On the contrary, they have divine power
to demolish strongholds.
2 CORINTHIANS 10:4

Sometimes spiritual growth can get a bit messy.

And to some degree, that's perfectly normal. Like a toddler who learns to walk by falling forward, we learn to "walk" with Christ through trial and error. In fact, that's often how we learn best.

Yet when an area of difficulty persists over time, it's possible we might be dealing with a spiritual stronghold.

WHAT'S A STRONGHOLD?

A few years ago, pastor Steve Berger taught an invaluable sermon series on this very subject. *(see "Winning the Mind Wars" sermon series at gracechapel.net)*

Here's my own definition, based on what I learned.

A STRONGHOLD IS...

A hellish pattern of thinking based on lies, distortions, and half truths that has become so deeply imbedded in your thoughts, attitudes, and emotions, it hinders your ability to believe God and live from your true identity in Christ. **It's allowing the devil's perspective to rule your thoughts in a given area!**

HOW DO YOU GET 'EM?

Strongholds are the direct result of NOT taking our thoughts captive to Christ. Sometimes they develop gradually over time, like the proverbial frog in the pot. Other times they develop instantly, through a traumatic circumstance the enemy exploits so he can sneak a lie or half-truth into our hearts.

165

**Once a stronghold is in place,
Satan uses it to attack our view of God
and ourselves from the *inside* out.**

Any time we allow unfiltered thoughts to rattle around inside our heads, the devil seizes the opportunity to slip in ideas that *sound* harmless but are actually quite destructive. Soon we're believing and acting on lies instead of truth, without even realizing it.

HOW DO YOU GET RID OF 'EM?

If spiritual strongholds are constructed of lies that get woven into the very fabric of how we think, how in heaven's name do you get rid of them?

You simply reverse the process.

**You smash a stronghold
by replacing its foundational lie
with an infinitely more powerful truth.**

Exposing a stronghold to the light of God's Word causes it to crumble to the ground as the hellish illusion it *always* was. Depending on how long that deception has been there, and how deeply it's been entrenched in your life, it may take some persistence to keep exposing that lie to the truth until it finally succumbs. It takes practice to learn the difference between God's truth and the devil's deceptions. Yet no matter how short or long the process—take heart.

God's truth always triumphs over deception!

Your part is simply to align your thinking with His Word—and renounce the lying logic of the world, the flesh, and the devil.

If you suspect you have a stronghold in your life, don't panic. Just start taking small deliberate steps of obedience forward, and God will be faithful to free you, as you allow the light of His truth to shine into the dark places of your heart.

1. **Start by memorizing this verse:** "We demolish arguments and every pretension that sets itself up against the knowledge of God, and we take captive every thought to make it obedient to Christ." 2 CORINTHIANS 10:5

2. **Then write down these three words:** Post these steps to smashing strongholds somewhere you'll notice them regularly.

   - **Recognize**
   - **Renounce**
   - **Renew**

Recognize

To recognize a hellish thought pattern in your life will require you to learn a new skill: **thinking about what you think about**.

How do you do that? You spend time in God's Word and compare your thoughts to His thoughts. It's that basic—and that amazing.

It can also be very helpful to talk over these comparisons with a trusted friend or mentor, since the *relational enzymes* of empathy and accountability help speed up the process.

The Bible tells us that as disciples of Jesus we've been given the mind of Christ. *Sit back and soak that in for a minute. Do you realize you have access to the mind of Christ at this very moment?* Whether you feel like it or not, you do!

It's as if you've been emailed a file that connects you with all the truth, love, and wisdom of Christ—but you only reap the benefits if you download it! Downloading God's Word regularly is a *must* for recognizing and smashing strongholds. Otherwise, the file does you very little good just sitting there in your inbox.

In the same way that bank tellers learn to recognize counterfeit bills by studying the real thing, we learn to recognize Satan's lies *by becoming so familiar with the cold hard cash of God's truth* that the enemy's lies look like cheap Monopoly money in comparison!

The next time you encounter a possible stronghold, ponder this question prayerfully before God.

**Do my thoughts about this situation
line up with the truth and love of Christ?**

If not, what about those thoughts smells fishy or counterfeit?

One thing that can be helpful in identifying strongholds is learning to recognize the enemy's **tells**. In a poker game, most players have an unconscious mannerism (or "tell") that lets their opponents know they have a good hand or are bluffing.

In your own life, you can become skilled at recognizing the enemy's **tells**. Start by working your way backward, and remembering what sort of tricks he's played on you before. Sometimes the devil gets cocky and overplays his hand, and if you pay attention you can catch him in the act!

If a certain sin tempts you beyond all reason, that's an area to keep an eye on. If you're flooded with unworthiness whenever you try to pray, there's a good chance the devil has something to do with it. Bear in mind, Satan is a big fat liar.

As Steve Berger often says, "If Satan's lips are moving, he's lying!"

Once the recognizing phase is complete, you're ready to move on to the next stronghold-smashing step.

Renounce

Imagine you're a detective who's captured a suspect for a serious crime. What do you do?

- *First you **arrest** him...*
- *Then you **question** him...*
- *If the **evidence** stacks up against him...*
- *You bring him to a **higher authority** for judgment...*
- *And if he's convicted, you **lock him up**!*

The same drill applies for suspected strongholds.

- *If they don't hold up against God's Word...*
- *If they prove themselves to be lies and enemies of God's truth...*
- *If they're potentially harmful to everyone they encounter...*

We arrest suspicious thoughts, question them, submit them to Christ for judgment—and say a firm NO to every thought He declares a lie!

Here's a simple one-two punch for "taking thoughts captive."

Grab a thought—and give it to God.

It will also be helpful to ask...

- *Lord, what do You think?*
- *Do any of my thoughts not line up with Yours?*
- *What does Your Word say about this situation?*
- *What thoughts, beliefs, or patterns need to be rerouted?*
- *How can I actively trust You where I've been believing a lie?*

Renew

Once God confirms that the pattern of thought is a lie, the next step is to *replace* it with a life-giving truth.

**The Bible calls this aspect of taking thoughts captive
"renewing your mind."**

So how do you renew your mind?

One of the best ways is to steep your mind in God's thoughts, like a teabag in a cup. Dislodging and destroying a deeply entrenched stronghold requires far more than a passing glance at truth. Full immersion in God's Word is your best weapon.

(and the longer you leave the teabag in the water, the stronger the tea!)

Of course, reading a verse a day is still a valuable habit. Any day we ingest God's Word is a good day. Yet if you suddenly discovered a tumor had been growing in your body for years, to the point that it's now affecting your daily health—you'd probably need more than just a few seconds of treatment a day!

The **PreScriptures** at the end of each mentoring milestone chapter are designed to help you with this immersion process. In his *Winning the Mind Wars* series, Steve Berger encourages believers to keep praying Scripture-based prayers as long as necessary to break a particular stronghold.

In other words, keep persevering to address the **root lie** of your stronghold *until that lie no longer has a (strong) hold on your daily life.*

SIX INCHES TO FREEDOM

At first blush, dealing with spiritual strongholds may sound intimidating.

Yet the more you understand about how your thoughts work and how God works, you'll see that you have much more control over which thoughts stay and which thoughts go than you realized. To quote an old saying: *You can't keep a bird from landing on your head, but you can keep it from building a nest in your hair!*

On the other hand, keep in mind that it's not uncommon for a stronghold that took years or even decades to build to take more than a day or two to demolish. Some fall quickly, while others take a while. Dealing with a deeply entrenched stronghold can sometimes feel like a journey of a thousand miles—and it's easy to become discouraged.

If that's your situation, don't lose heart.

Your perseverance WILL pay off!

Ultimately, the enemy's evil works will come to nothing, and God's good work in your life will stand the test of eternity.

Here's a helpful phrase to remember when dealing with strongholds...

Six inches to freedom.

The battle to stay stronghold-free is largely a battle for our minds. And the width of the average human brain is (you guessed it) six inches.

So you *don't* have a thousand miles to go.

**You only have to travel
six inches to freedom!**

But what a *huge* difference those six inches make.

Many people who attempt to break through strongholds stop short about *two* inches. *They don't realize how close they are to victory.* Imagine the misery of living your whole life only TWO inches from your promised land?

Don't be that person!

Persevere a little longer. Lean into God's strength a little longer. Immerse yourself in the Word, surround yourself with godly supporters, believe you are who God says you are, and press through those last two inches to victory.

Six. Inches. To. Freedom.

Years from now, you'll be oh-so-grateful you did!

WATCH YOUR THOUGHTS
by Frank Outlaw

Watch your **THOUGHTS**,

for they become words.

Watch your **WORDS**,

for they become actions.

Watch your **ACTIONS**,

for they become habits.

Watch your **HABITS**,

for they become character.

Watch your **CHARACTER**,

for it becomes your

DESTINY.

3 WAYS TO OBEY

PONDER
---

1. **Have you ever heard of strongholds before?** In your own words, describe what a stronghold is and why they need to be demolished.

2. **Is there an area of thought or action that keeps tripping you up on a regular basis?** Spend a few minutes reviewing the scenario that keeps repeating itself in your life. What thoughts go through your mind? What triggers them? What are the negative consequences?

PRACTICE
---

1. **WRITE:** Spend five to ten minutes journaling about this pattern of thought or action and how it has negatively affected your life. Ask God to reveal the lies you have believed, and the corresponding truth He wants to replace them with.

2. **CREATE:** Set aside thirty to sixty minutes and write out your own personalized Scripture prayer to address the stronghold in your life that needs to be demolished. List the lie or lies you've believed and ask God to give you specific verse(s) to address each one. Then personalize the verses in the form of a prayer.

   If you find this process overwhelming, invite a friend or mentor to help you look up the verses and write out the Scripture prayer. Then once it's finished, you'll have a built-it encourager and prayer partner to help you smash that stronghold!

3. **DEMOLISH:** Pray your personalized Scripture prayer (or of any of the *PreScriptures* in this book) daily, weekly, or as often as needed to smash that pesky stronghold to smithereens. Don't become discouraged if it doesn't fall to the ground immediately. (think of how long it took to build it...) Keep shining the light of God's Truth on your heart, mind, and emotions, and before you know it that hellish pattern of thought WILL crumble!

PRAY

Breaking the Strong Hold...of Strongholds!

The enemy of our souls has been fully defeated by the cross and resurrection of Jesus Christ. The only "authority" left to him is what he leeches off God's people through deception, convincing them to think and act in a way contrary to the truth. These lies and half-truths, once believed, gain a "strong hold" on our patterns of thought, feeling, and action. Yet the good news is, they AREN'T true and they CAN be broken through the recognizing, renouncing, and renewing power of God's Word!

STRONGHOLDS
PreScripture

Lord Jesus, You have already beaten and disarmed Satan through Your death and resurrection, making a public mockery of his lies, his schemes, and every evil work that opposes Your truth, love, and righteous rule and reign.	**Colossians 2:13-15**
Thank you that we do not wage war according to the flesh, but according to the Spirit, and that You've given us authority to demolish satanic strongholds wherever we find them in Your name and by Your power.	**2 Corinthians 10:3-5**
Thank you that I do not have to conform to the pattern of this world, but can be transformed by the renewing of my mind, which enables me to recognize Your will when I see it.	**Romans 12:1-2**
Thank you that Your truth will set me free, and that the devil must flee when I resist him in Your name and submit to You!	**John 8:32** **James 4:7**
Thank you that godly repentance leaves no regret and You gladly give me the mind of Christ to replace the lies I have believed.	**2 Corinthians 7:10** **I Corinthians 2:16**
Thank you that in Christ I am free to think on what is true, noble, right, pure, lovely, admirable, excellent, and praiseworthy, and my future now flows from Your truth and NOT the lies of the enemy!	**Philippians 4:8** **Proverbs 4:23**

SIP 25

PASSIONATE PURPOSE

God never loses sight of the treasure
which He has placed in our earthen vessels.
CHARLES SPURGEON

When the house is on fire,
don't tell me what your spiritual gift is.
Just grab a hose and put out the fire.
ANDY STANLEY

Every apprentice of Jesus is *also* His ambassador.

Day by day, week by week, and year by year, He delights in revealing His glory and extending His grace through salt-of-the-earth disciples like you. Whatever your current circumstances, your daily decision to love and obey the Risen Savior reveals you are *already* a world-changer.

DISCOVERING YOUR DESIGN

Yet deep down, we also long to know, *Does God have a particular purpose for me, something I'm uniquely created to do?*

We each have at least three areas of uniqueness—**talents, spiritual gifts, and life experiences**—that God flows through to fulfill our purpose or calling. Notice I didn't say our gifts and talents *determine* our calling, because God can use our gifts in any combination He chooses, in any given season.

Let's examine the three areas of uniqueness we each possess.

Talents

Often we don't even recognize out abilities as talents because we take them for granted: *Aww, that's no big deal...anyone could do that!*

So then, what *is* a talent?

A talent is a natural aptitude or skill that comes easier
for you than it does for the average person.

173

If you're not sure what your talents are, try asking a couple of your closest friends what they think you do well. Whether you agree or disagree, their answers will be good food for thought. After all, your friends see your life from an angle you never could.

Spiritual Gifts

For clarity's sake, what is a spiritual gift?

**Spiritual gifts are manifestations of God's character and power
given to believers by the Holy Spirit
for the building up of the church
and the display of His glory.**

That's a pretty exhilarating thought, when you stop and think about it. Yet when spiritual gifts come up in conversation, people's reactions tend to be mixed.

- *Wow, that's so interesting, I'd love to know what mine are!*
- *Sounds great, but I probably don't even have any.*
- *That spiritual gift stuff sounds kinda weird to me.*
- *I took a test a while back—turns out I only have the "wimpy" gifts.*

Sadly, many believers leave their spiritual gifts unopened. This often happens due to fear, lack of information, or both.
Don't let that happen to you!
If you can open a present on Christmas morning, you can discover your spiritual gifts.

❏ **Open the box.**

I Corinthians 12:7

Thank God in advance, tear that box open, and look inside your heart to see what gifts God has *already* placed there. Start paying attention to what motivates you, how God prompts you to reach out to others, and what tends to bear the most fruit. You may even want to take a spiritual gifts assessment to help speed up the process.

(see Appendix for "Spiritual Growth Reading List" - Spiritual Gifts)

❑ **When in doubt, read the instructions!**

I Corinthians 12-14
Romans 12:3-8
Ephesians 4:1-16

Ever notice how long you fumble around with gadgets on Christmas morning before breaking down and reading the instructions? These great "instruction" passages will help get you started. (see if you relate to any of the gifts they list...)

❑ **Try it out—and get feedback.**

2 Timothy 1:6

Think something might be your gift? Then give it try! There's nothing like real-life experience to fan a new gift into flame.

Giving your gift a test run will also help you discover...

1. Do I have ability in this area?
2. Do I see fruit in people's lives as a result?

Proverbs 11:14

It's also great to get feedback from leaders, co-workers, or those you minister with. Again, others can see things we can't, so asking them often helps shed light on the process.

(again, see Appendix for resources)

❑ **Give it away!**

I Peter 4:10
Matthew 11:28-30

Once you've opened your gifts, read the instructions, tried them out, and gotten feedback—you're ready to start giving them away to others! Look for opportunities in your daily life to lovingly serve those around you. The very best way to refine and strengthen a spiritual gift is to *use* it.

Life Experience

Your third area of uniqueness is life experience.

No one in all of history has ever lived out the exact combination of experiences you have. That's why you can see a facet of God's glory from a completely unique vantage point!

That said, you also share certain kinds of experiences in common with others. For example, any woman who's carried a child for nine months and given birth shares an instant connection with every other woman who's ever had that experience. If a woman merely mentions she's pregnant, she's suddenly surrounded by fellow moms who can "totally relate."

You may connect over **positive experiences,** such as shared hometown, ethnicity, family background, schools, hobbies, interests, friends in common, years married, number of kids, career path, or ministry passions.

Or you may connect over more **challenging experiences**, such as childhood trauma, losses, learning challenges, insecurities, discouragement, depression, anxiety, financial challenges, traumatic events, illness, injury, or grief.

While it's great to connect over fun things we have in common, we tend to shy away from mentioning the more unsettling areas of life. Yet being real about the difficult things God has brought us through is often the very thing He uses to build a deeper heart connection between us and those around us. As the saying goes, He's oh-so-capable of turning your test into a *testimony* and your mess into a *message!*

Another benefit of life experience (both positive and negative) is how it fuels our **passion**. Those who've gone through the heartbreak of bankruptcy tend to have a passion for helping people get out of debt. Those who've struggled with weight loss often have a passion for healthy nutrition and fitness. Those who love art, music, sports, or travel often have a deep and abiding passion for their favorite pastime.

Also, the more we yield ourselves to God, He often deepens our passion in specific areas. Have you ever been watching the news or crossed paths with someone in heartbreaking need and heard God whisper, *I want you to do something about that.* And in that moment, you find yourself fired up by a Holy Spirit passion you might never have felt on your own.

C.S. LEWIS: *Friendship is born at the moment when one person says to another "What! You too? I thought I was the only one."*

FREDERICK BUECHNER: *The place God calls you to is the place where your deep gladness and the world's deep hunger meet.*

RECOGNIZING YOUR PURPOSE

A few years ago, I stumbled onto the practice of helping people view their talents, spiritual gifts, and life experiences simultaneously—which as a culture is something we rarely do.

We tend to think about talents when choosing a hobby, spiritual gifts when studying the Bible, and life experience when we're filling out a resume or venting to our friends that we "just can't catch a break."

**We rarely pause to ponder
our talents, spiritual gifts,
and life experience all at once.**

This *a la carte* approach to life keeps us from catching a bird's eye view of how God is truly working. Our tunnel-vision focus blinds us to how skillfully our Shepherd is weaving those seemingly random twists and turns of our lives into purposeful patterns of growth, tenderly equipping and positioning us to be *exactly* the kind of person He's calling us to be.

Nor do we notice Him molding us into the image of Jesus in such a wonderful one-of-a-kind way that we're becoming more and more "ourselves" than ever before.

Without that *bird's eye view*, we may be tempted to think God has no real purpose for our lives. Yet often, when we take the time to prayerfully ponder all three areas of gifting at once, patterns of clarity and purpose we've never noticed before start rising to the surface.

For that reason, I suggest setting aside a few minutes to write down your talents, spiritual gifts, and significant life experiences all in one place. Feel free to download my free resource for this purpose. *(see Appendix for "Fanning the Flame" worksheet)*

Once you've got it all down on paper, stop and pray.

Ask God to give you wisdom, clarity, and the eyes to see what He's invested in you from *His* perspective—trusting that He will.

Then take a few minutes to reread your list with fresh eyes. If you notice any recurring patterns or themes, jot them down in the margins of your list. Then ask God to reveal any **next steps of obedience** He wants you to take.

When I've taught workshops on this subject, I've been amazed at how much clarity can be gained through this process! For some it's a flash of "Aha!" revelation, while others experience a gentle sense of "Hmm, I never thought of it that way before—maybe I'll try this." Either way, as we're faithful to **show up** and **pay attention**, we position ourselves to hear God's voice and receive His guidance. I recommend repeating this process in different seasons of life (as God leads) as a way of being a good steward of all He's entrusted to you.

The One who made you *does* have passionate purpose for your life—whether it's a particular task to accomplish, core principles to live out, or simply being the most obedient one-of-a-kind original you can possibly be!

LIVING YOUR PURPOSE

After you look at the bird's eye view of what God has entrusted to you, my advice for discovering and living out your passionate purpose is pretty basic.

**Start by obeying what you understand so far.
Then "lather, rinse, repeat."**

Seriously. That's it.

Obey the clear commands of the Bible, as best you can. Love God, love others, and put into action any specific guidance you believe He gives you. Do this with all your heart.

That's it.

Your purpose isn't behind door number one, two, or three.

Your purpose emanates from the very heart of God—which is why drawing near to Him is so exciting. He's overflowing with goodness and full of surprises. *And He always has a heart to give to you and through you.* So it only makes sense that the more you hang out with Him, and do what He tells you—the more you'll hear what's in His heart for you!

Whether God reveals His purposeful direction for your life inch by inch or all at once, there's incredible peace in simply obeying what you *do* know and trusting Him with what you *don't.*

For example, after decades of doing the above, I'm now confident that my purpose involves being a passionate disciple of Jesus, a mentor of millennials, and an equipper of thirsty women of all ages. Over the years, God has confirmed these areas of purpose to my heart dozens of times. Yet there are many and varied ways He leads me to walk them out in any given season.

For almost ten years, I just loved the girl in front of me and let Jesus do the mentoring. Then gradually He began planting the idea of speaking into my heart. Then writing bubbled to the surface. As I started doing that, He opened my eyes to the need for more women to invest in millennials, which led to Him revealing His heart for women of all ages who've never experienced being mentored themselves.

As I've acted on what God has shown me so far, and listened for His next instructions, slowly but surely my purpose has unfolded. I can't tell you exactly what it will look like in five, ten, or twenty years—but I *can* tell you God has worked certain kingdom truths so deeply into my soul that wherever I go, whatever I do, they come pouring out of me into the lives of those I meet.

The same will be true of you.

You have a handful of people you "do life" with—your friends, family, neighbors, co-workers, and acquaintances. God has given you *influence* in those people's lives.

The Bible calls these people our **oikos** or "extended household."

- *Start with your oikos.*
- *Care deeply about them.*
- *Pour God's love into them.*
- *Lay down your life for them.*

And as you take one faithful step at a time—*your passionate kingdom purpose will unfold!*

3 WAYS TO OBEY

PONDER

1. **What are some of your talents?** Is there anything you love to do so much you'd be willing to do it for free?

   Do you have any idea what your spiritual gifts might be? When you feel especially close to God, what sorts of things do you tend to do quite (super) naturally?

2. **What causes or people groups are you passionate about and why?** If you could make a lasting difference in one aspect of the world, what would it be?

3. **What sort of life experience have you had (positive or negative) that tends to bond you with others who've had a similar experience?** How do you envision God using this experience to impact others in the future?

PRACTICE

1. **Get a copy of *Discover Your Spiritual Gifts the Network Way* by Bruce L. Bugbee and complete one of the four spiritual gifts assessments.** Then bring the results to your next friend or mentor get-together to share and discuss.

2. **Pick one of your spiritual gifts and ask God to give you some creative ideas on how to practice using it.** This week, use this spiritual gift to intentionally bless someone. Discuss and pray about the results with a friend or mentor. Repeat this process for 2-4 weeks until you feel you've gotten the hang of using that particular gift to bless others.

3. **Grab a sheet of paper and draw a line down the center from top to bottom.** In the left-hand column list who's in your *oikos* (the 8-15 people you "do life" with) in this current season. In the right-hand column, brainstorm ways you could serve each person by using your spiritual gifts. Pick one idea and do it this week!

PRAY

Breaking the "I Have No Purpose" Stronghold!

In this confusing, sin-stained world, it's easy to become convinced our lives don't make much difference one way or the other. Yet as disciples of Christ we don't have to believe that hellish lie. The truth is, God has kingdom purpose for your life that fits beautifully into His Master Plan—sometimes in ways you can clearly see, and other times in ways you won't fully understand til heaven. Yet either way, it is still God's will for us to walk in intentional, passionate, faith-filled purpose!

PASSIONATE PURPOSE
PreScripture

Lord, thank you that You have good plans for my life,
to give me a future and a hope.
Though I don't know all You have in store for me,
I know that as I make prayerful plans
and move forward in faith,
You will order my steps in the right direction.

Jeremiah 29:11
Proverbs 16:9
Proverbs 3:5-6

I say NO to the enemy's lie that I have nothing
to contribute and will never amount to anything, and say
a wholehearted YES to Your glorious inheritance for me!

Psalm 71:11-13
Nehemiah 4:1-6
Psalm 16:5-6

Thank you for giving me everything I need
for life and godliness, including all the resources,
abilities, and valuable life experience I need
to live out the purpose You intend for me.

2 Peter 1:3

Thank you that You use even my worst experiences
and deepest hurts to restore me, equip me,
bless others, and bring glory to Your name.

Romans 8:28

You also have given me specific spiritual gifts in Christ
to strengthen and encourage my fellow believers
and show Your glory to those who don't yet know You.
Thank you for clearly explaining in Your Word
how I can personally be part of that!

I Corinthians 12
Romans 12:4-8
Ephesians 4:11-13
I Peter 4:10

As I walk out Your will for my life step by step,
I commit myself to letting Your truth and love
pour through me by Your Spirit in any way You wish.

Matthew 22:36-40
I Corinthians 13:13
Psalm 43:3

Thank you for including me, equipping me, calling me Your
masterpiece, preparing good works for me to do,
and teaching me to walk in passionate purpose with You!

Ephesians 2:10

SIP 26

INVESTING
YOUR INHERITANCE

*Transformation in the world happens
when people are healed and start investing in other people.*
MICHAEL W. SMITH

*An inheritance is what you leave with people.
A legacy is what you leave in them.*
CRAIG D. LOUNSBROUGH

God has given you a glorious inheritance.

As a king's daughter who's put her trust in Christ, you've been given a new identity, adopted into a new family, taught a new way of life, and granted citizenship in His kingdom where you'll reign with Him forever. *And that kingdom way of life began the moment you said yes to Jesus.*

Your kingdom inheritance is filled to overflowing with life, love, and truth. And now it's time to pass it along!

RIVER VS. POND

God wants His people to be rivers, not ponds.

What's the difference?

For starters, a pond has no outlet. Water flows in, but never pours out. That's why ponds tend to stagnate.

A river, on the other hand, is a raucous riot of life. River water dances downstream, hurling itself from rock to rock, as it races its way toward the sea. Rivers bring life. That's why civilizations have always sprung up around them.

**Ponds are pretty,
but rivers are givers!**

That's also how it works in our spiritual lives. If we always drink in but never pour out, something goes terribly wrong in our soul. It soon begins to stagnate, because it has no outlet.

On the other hand, if we freely pour out the truth, love, and encouragement we've received, we become like life-giving rivers. Soon growth begins springing up all around us, both in areas we intentionally planted *and* some we didn't!

The One who fills us with *living water* is calling us to be rivers, not ponds.

BEGIN WITH THE END IN MIND

Stop for a moment and imagine yourself deeply rooted in Jesus.

Picture your spiritual foundation built so solidly on Christ that He's squarely at the center of everything you think, feel, say, and do.

Then imagine yourself interacting with Him in such daily peace and confidence that even as you go through life's frustrations and trials, you can't seem to stop growing, learning, loving, and giving—nor would you even want to if you could!

Now picture God nudging you to invest in one of His daughters.

It's possible she's part of your regular circle already—a friend, neighbor, coworker, or acquaintance. Can you see her yet, is she coming into focus?

Yes, there she is.

Now, remember those struggles that used to plague you?

Those broken places in your heart you thought could never be healed? Well, she's got 'em too. She's also got a fair amount of maturing to do, just like you did. And she needs a Jesus-with-skin-on friend to help her.

- *What if you could do for her what someone else did for you?*
- *What if your story is the very thing she needs to hear?*
- *What if God has prepared you for such a time as this?*

After all, you already have a fair idea of the kind of support she'll need. Some spiritual scaffolding, a listening ear, and someone to point her to Jesus. *So what if you took those first few awkward steps forward—and let Jesus knit your hearts together in a life-giving way?*

Now picture this same girl two, five, or even ten years from now. Picture her deeply rooted in Jesus, with a clear sense of identity and an ever-deepening faith that spills over into love and service of those around her. Then imagine her meeting someone a few years younger than her—a girl who's in need of the same kind of Jesus investment she experienced with you. Before you know it, they'll be walking a few coffee-cup miles together—just as you did with her and someone did with you.

Finally, picture the faces of your spiritual grandchildren, two, three, and four generations into the future—many of whom have been birthed and brought up before your very eyes by those you personally loved into maturity.

Are you catching the vision?

Investing our inheritance
IS the abundant life!

Instead of desperately clutching our inheritance, we can learn to freely invest what we've been freely given. Whether here or in heaven (or both), I believe at least *part* of our reward will include the astonished realization of how many lives Jesus has transformed through our simple "Yes Lord."

(that and the gracious way He *accelerates* our own growth in the process!)

So this is our "disciple sips" journey—*the Great Commission with skin on.* This is the rich, flavorful, full-circle kingdom of God at its redemptive best.

This is how we invest our inheritance—
and leave a Jesus legacy!

3 WAYS TO OBEY

PONDER
---

1. **Would you say your current life leans more toward the river or pond analogy?** If the pond, do you see any areas where you could become more intentional about receiving from or pouring into others?

2. **Have you ever thought of yourself as a future discipler?** How does it feel to picture yourself investing in others what Jesus has invested in you? What appeals to you and what sounds scary?

PRACTICE
---

1. **Pick one area of your life and apply the "be a river, not a pond" principle to it.** If you're stuck for ideas, you can always volunteer at a youth center, homeless shelter, or soup kitchen. Sometimes just getting in the habit of serving *in general* can spur more *specific ideas* of how you could serve using your spiritual gifts.

2. **What's one small step you could take toward preparing yourself to disciple others?** This doesn't need to be complicated, just intentional.

   For example, you could...

   - Write down a couple verses to build your confidence—try Matthew 28:18-20, 2 Corinthians 3:5-6, or 2 Timothy 2:2.

   - Ask God to *prepare the heart* of the person He wants you to disciple and *lead you to her* in His timing.

   - Invite a younger believer to coffee and swap Jesus stories while sipping your favorite drinks. *If you have fun, try it again within the next month!*

PRAY

Embracing a "Jesus Legacy" Lifestyle!

Christ has given us a glorious inheritance. He's transferred us from the kingdom of darkness to the kingdom of light, given us a new identity, adopted us into His family, empowered us with His authority, and assured us of eternity in heaven with Him. He's also offered us the privilege of investing our inheritance in others by walking them through the same transformation process we've experienced—thus bringing our own redemption story full-circle and leaving a Jesus legacy!

INVESTING YOUR INHERITANCE
PreScripture

Thank you, Lord, for my glorious inheritance in Christ!	Psalm 16:5-6
You have poured Your truth and love into my life so freely that lies, brokenness, shame, insecurity, pride, fear, and hopelessness are losing their grip on me.	I John 4:16 Colossians 3:7
And truth, wholeness, joy, peace, confidence, healing, hope, and fruitfulness are becoming my "new normal" more and more each day.	Galatians 5:22-23 2 Corinthians 5:17
Thank you that my future in heaven, where I will enjoy the beauty of Your kingdom and rule and reign with You, starts here and now today as You teach me Your kingdom ways!	Revelation 21:4 John 14:2 Romans 8:17 Matthew 10:7-8
I choose this day to obey Your command to "go and make disciples" out of loving obedience to Jesus and a heartfelt desire to see others experience the genuine transformation and glorious inheritance I've been so freely given.	Matthew 28:18-20 John 7:37-38 Matthew 10:8 Luke 10:9 Ephesians 5:2
Thank you that You've strengthened, equipped, empowered, and commissioned me to invest the gospel in others.	Acts 1:8
In Jesus' Name, I commit to investing my inheritance in the next generation of believers—	2 Timothy 3:16-17 Psalm 16:5-6
one conversation, one sip, and one legacy-filled latte at a time!	2 Timothy 2:2

EPILOGUE

What's Your Next Step?

Wow, I can't believe our DiscipleSips journey is almost over...

I truly admire you for facing your fears and opening your heart to a new way of thinking and living. Making disciples is something you absolutely CAN do!

So what's your NEXT step?

Here are a few more ideas to get you started...

1. FILL UP: Find your own mentor

❑ Ask God to provide a mentor (or peer mentor) if you need one.

❑ Ask _____ to walk thru the *Mentoring Milestones* with you.

2. SET UP: Set some "loving limits"

❑ **AVAILABILITY**: ❑ Weekly ❑ Every other week ❑ Monthly

❑ **MENTORING STYLE**: ❑ Coffee chats ❑ Do a Bible study ❑ As-you-go

❑ **PRAYER PARTNER**: Ask _____ to be your prayer partner.

3. POUR OUT: Find a mentee

❑ Ask God: Lord, is _____ mentor-ready yet?

❑ If YES, invite _____ to coffee this week/month

❑ If NO, keep praying: *Lord, I trust You to guide me to the young woman You want me to invest in.*

It only takes a **moment**...to start moving **forward**!

ONLINE APPENDIX

An online appendix for DiscipleSips may be found at:
KimAldrich.com/DiscipleSipsResources

Here are the resources you will find there...

❑ **Free PDF—8 Mentoring Milestones** (Sips 19-26 for mentees)

❑ **Back Pocket Basics Worksheet** (Section 3)

❑ **Setting Loving Limits—Mentor Worksheet** (Sip 13)

❑ **Setting Loving Limits—Mentor + Mentee Worksheet** (Sip 13)

❑ **Who's in My *Oikos*? Worksheet** (Sip 14, Sip 25)

❑ **Mentor-Ready Checklist** (Sip 14)

❑ **Mentoring Milestones Checklist** (Section 3, Section 4)

❑ **Who Am I in Christ?** (Sip 19)

❑ **Fanning the Flame Worksheet** (Sip 25)

❑ **Spiritual Growth Reading List** (by subject)

TRIBE — A Community of Disciplers

If you're ready to **drink in** and **pour out**
Jesus' truth and love to the point of overflowing...

why not join a
Holy-Spirit empowered tribe of women
who are learning to do the same thing?

I get a caffeine-free burst of adrenaline just thinking about it!

Join us at

kimaldrich.com

*(aka: **DiscipleSips.com**)*

Check out the free resources, shareables, and other
DiscipleSips goodies you won't wanna miss! ☺

TO BOOK KIM AT YOUR NEXT EVENT...

website: kimaldrich.com/speaking
email: kim@kimaldrich.com

FOR PERSONAL OR GROUP COACHING WITH KIM...

website: kimaldrich.com/coaching
email: kim@kimaldrich.com

71046475R00117

Made in the USA
Columbia, SC
24 August 2019